Praise for *The Authentic Actor*

"Michael Laskin is a shining light, a steady positive example, a genius; this book is a true gift. *The Authentic Actor* presents the knowledge and acumen of a hugely talented actor and a true teacher who has been 'in the rooms', felt the victories, and weathered the no-thank-you's. Michael's words compass, instruct, probe, and unerringly point us home, especially when we forget where true north really is. He firmly leads us to artistry, and ultimately to ourselves."
— JEFFREY TAMBOR, actor, *Transparent, Arrested Development, The Larry Sanders Show*

"This book is fuel for the Long Haul of an acting career. Laskin examines business, craft, and commitment in a direct and extremely useful manner. Musicians, athletes, and politicians (really) can find a lot to think about here as well."
— JOHN SAYLES, writer / director, *Lone Star, Eight Men Out, Matewan*

"Laskin singularly defines himself as a master artist and a master teacher. He presents real gold, real vitality, and an appreciation and passion for the art form that is sublime and utterly contagious... belongs to a tiny handful of books that should be indispensable to actors both old and new."
— RON PERLMAN, actor, *Hellboy, Sons of Anarchy, Beauty and the Beast*

"Michael's book speaks to the working actor, the aspiring student, and anyone interested in the techniques and common-sense approaches to our craft. He brings accurate insights and sharp observation to the work that are often lacking [elsewhere]. His knowledge and experience are balanced with a quick wit and an appreciation of the vagaries of our industry."
— ALFRED MOLINA, actor, *Magnolia, The Da Vinci Code, An Education, As You Like It, Enchanted April*

"Laskin's book is much more than a treatise on what lies beneath this acting thing. It is a 'must read' for any artist in pursuit of that one truth that will pull them through anything with which they may be confronted on their journey toward true success."
— DAVID STRATHAIRN, Academy Award–nominated actor, *Lincoln, Good Night and Good Luck, Eight Men Out, L.A. Confidential*

"Passionate and smart. Michael works with several of our clients, and simply put: I trust Michael Laskin."
— MARSHA MCMANUS, Principal Entertainment talent manager, Seth Rogen, Jim Parsons, Tom Wilkinson, Andy Serkis

"We are *crazy* to do what we do. We kind of have to be. But our crazy can produce more self-doubt and insecurity than actual work. That's why I call Laskin 'The Captain'. Michael's voice is the one you *want* to hear in your head. Calm, kind, with the sort of rooted confidence that soaks in and becomes your own. *The Authentic Actor* gives you all that and more. 'The Captain' steers your crazy to a place where it can really work for you."
— STORM LARGE, actor; playwright; musician, Pink Martini; author, *Crazy Enough*; television personality, *Rock Star: Supernova*

"A hugely valuable guide for anyone interested in the craft and commerce of the acting profession, primarily because the author himself is authentic. Laskin has been there and done it many times over, so his down-to-earth insights into what the life (and a lifetime) of being an actor entail contain the truth and wisdom that money can't buy."
— JIM PIDDOCK, actor, *Best in Show*, *Independence Day*; writer / producer, *Family Tree* (HBO), *Too Much Sun*

"A clever and insightful gift to student and professional alike. In it, with his years of work and experience as both actor and teacher, Michael probes deeply into the truth and mystery of the craft, truly showing how art can be created through hard work, faith, and — above all — honesty."
— CHARLIE HAID, actor, *Hill Street Blues*, *Altered States*; DGA Award–winning director, *ER*, *NYPD Blue*, *Breaking Bad*, *Nip/Tuck*

"An essential read for actors and other creative professionals. From the business side to the creative, Laskin's wisdom is based around discovering the most powerful tool you have: being yourself. *The Authentic Actor* is not another 'how to act' book, but rather one about how to [ensure] your own unique talents aren't held back. Easy to read; fresh and perfect for the 21st century."
— ERIN CORRADO, OneMovieOurViews.com

"... bypasses the BS and strips away the superfluous... focused, original, and real. An experienced and respected professional actor offers examples from his own career, communicating his ideas with clarity and assurance. Filled with wisdom won by years of hard work and dedication, *The Authentic Actor* goes to the top of my list of books I happily recommend."
— TOMMY G. KENDRICK, SAG-AFTRA actor; producer, Actors Talk podcast

"Laskin's lucid, unpretentious prose lifts the veil of a hitherto ephemeral and mysterious craft, thereby connecting with actor and 'civilian' alike. He presents his clear insights with something like joy. If this small jewel of a book doesn't help you become a better actor, it will at least help you become a better person."
— HECTOR ELIZONDO, Emmy Award–winning actor, *Chicago Hope*, *Pretty Woman*, *Tortilla Soup*, *The Princess Diaries*

"A no-B.S. approach to acting. Laskin is blunt and truthful; he sugarcoats nothing and preaches no magic method to becoming a better actor. What he does teach you is a mindset that will guide you in becoming the best performer that you can be. Overflowing with straightforward advice, practical tips, and simple exercises, *The Authentic Actor* is as important and valuable to an actor as a hammer is to a carpenter."
— FORRIS DAY Jr., actor; writer / reviewer, *Scared Stiff Reviews*, ScriptMag.com; podcast host, Coffee Shop Conversations

"Offers the tools to walk into a room with confidence in who you are and what you uniquely bring to each role, seamlessly merging character and self to bring authenticity and heart to the material... changed the way I broke down my auditions. Since Michael's coaching, I've been working consistently... long awaited!"
— CAMILLA LUDDINGTON, actor, *Grey's Anatomy*, *Tomb Raider* video game

The Authentic

ACTOR

THE ART AND BUSINESS OF BEING YOURSELF

Michael Laskin

Edited by Jana Branch

MICHAEL WIESE PRODUCTIONS

Published by Michael Wiese Productions
12400 Ventura Blvd. #1111
Studio City, CA 91604
(818) 379-8799, (818) 986-3408 (FAX)
mw@mwp.com
www.mwp.com

Cover design by Johnny Ink. www.johnnyink.com
Cover image by Rena Colette Photography, www.renacolette.com
Copyeditor: Ross Plotkin
Printed by McNaughton & Gunn

Manufactured in the United States of America

The author acknowledges the copyright owners of the following motion pictures and television series from which single frames have been used in this book for purposes of commentary, criticism, and scholarship under the Fair Use Doctrine.

21 Jump Street
Bounce
Eight Men Out
Iron Will
Limbo
The Man Who Captured Eichmann
Medium
Mini's First Time
Poodle Springs
Seinfeld
Winchell

Library of Congress Cataloging-in-Publication Data

Laskin, Michael, 1951–
The Authentic Actor: The Art and Business of Being Yourself / by Michael Laskin.
pages cm
Includes bibliographical references.
ISBN 978-1-61593-222-1
1. Acting. I. Title.
PN2061.L37 2015
792.02'8--dc23
2014038309

For all Authentic Actors at every stage of their journey —
those just discovering the call,
those in the thick of it,
those renewing their creative vows,
and
those who need to be reminded of their own talent.

It's not show business. It's human business.

CONTENTS

1

Today's Authentic Actor

2

Who Are You?

3

What Do You Know?

4
Success Factors

5
The Audition

6

The Art of Career

7

The Business of Life

FOREWORD

Disclosure: The author is my friend. My good friend.

Further disclosure: The author is a former student of my acting workshop that I called "Not for Pishers" (i.e., experienced) and was a shining light and a steady positive example, sitting there at the Santa Monica Playhouse on those long Monday evenings.

More: The author produced my first college speaking engagement and launched me on a lecture tour of the United States.

Too many years ago, I auditioned for a role in TNT's *The Man Who Captured Eichmann*, starring the great Robert Duvall. I didn't get the part. I suspect I underwhelmed "Bobby" and the director. Many weeks later, as it happens in this business we fondly call "show," I got a phone call from my agent: "They want you on a plane tomorrow for Buenos Aires." The actor they had cast, Peter Riegert, had to bow out at the last moment, and I was to replace him. This was a better role than the one I'd auditioned for; this was the head of the Mossad, the Israeli intelligence agency. This was the man who'd engineered the capture of Adolf Eichmann in Argentina.

Cut to: on the set of the film, my character's meeting with David Ben-Gurion (the Prime Minister of Israel) to set the secret capture in motion. Seated next to me on the set was "Dr. Klein," played by Michael Laskin, the author of this book. I remember we had to sit under those lights for what seemed an eternity to begin the scene. Waiting. Waiting. Michael and I and a dead ringer for David Ben-Gurion, just sitting there in complete silence. I knew I was "under the gun," as it were; I was the new guy — the replacement — and Duvall was on his way down to have a look-see.

We heard a door open at the rear of the soundstage, followed by a number of determined and measured steps to a producer's chair in front of the video monitor. I began to get very nervous, and it was then I looked at Michael and gave a panicked shrug of my shoulders. I can remember what he did to this day. He looked me straight in the eyes, dropped his chin, and gave me the Michael Laskin "nod" — this was going to be a snap, and all would be well.

The scene went without a hitch and rather well, as first takes go. The director yelled "cut," and Michael gave me the nod again. We were home free. We heard the measured steps again and the closing of the stage door — I was "approved."

In Hebrew, what Michael did for me that day is called a *mitzvah*. And who Michael is — is called in Yiddish a *mensch*. Both *mensch* and *mitzvah* are at hand throughout the following pages. Here is the knowledge and acumen of a hugely talented actor and a teacher who, as the kids say, has "been there, done that" — all accomplished with an ease and the same positive presence I witnessed those years ago on the soundstage in Buenos Aires.

Acting classes can be dicey. Too often they are led by a teacher who is demanding a specific style and a strict, unwavering approach to the work. Neophyte actors end up spending too many hours, too much effort, and too much cash in order to PLEASE the teacher, who is insisting on a prescribed set of codes and style. What follows in these chapters is FREEDOM and a technique for the young actor to mine his uniqueness — his purpose, his authenticity. Michael, and this book, are all about authenticity.

The author has a love for actors and the art of acting, plus an understanding of what it takes to fashion a career. He has been "in the rooms." He has felt the victories and weathered the no-thank-you's. But what surfaces constantly in these chapters is his love of acting for its own sake. In his hands, a career is not the number of jobs, nor the salary, nor the billing. The pay is the doing, the making — the act, if you will, of acting in and of itself.

Like Michael, I have taught acting classes. Many students succeed, but far too many give up and settle for easier and "more comfortable rooms" and predictable lives. Michael has a chapter on what keeps actors from success. He asks: What is the "story" that prevents us from achieving our goals? From success?

In classical mythology we learn about the hero and his journey. And in every journey comes the call to the hero's purpose, to his true self. And woe to the man or woman who fails to heed that beckoning. And for the call to be answered and the journey to be underway, there must be a guide. This is the Mentor.

The mentor and his guidance mark this book throughout. Michael Laskin, his firm and positive grip under our arms as he leads us to artistry and ultimately to ourselves, is the genius of this book. He is a true teacher. This book is a true gift. Michael's words compass, instruct, probe, and unerringly point us home, especially when we forget where true north really is.

JEFFREY TAMBOR
New York, New York

Jeffrey Tambor is a classically trained actor known for his iconic roles on television (*The Larry Sanders Show*, *Arrested Development*, *Transparent*), film (*...And Justice for All*, *Meet Joe Black*, *The Hangover*), and Broadway (*Glengarry Glen Ross*, *Sly Fox*). In addition to his 45-year acting career, he is also a noted acting teacher and lecturer.

ACKNOWLEDGMENTS

First and foremost, I thank my students and coaching clients, who teach me lessons on a regular basis. While much of this book is based on my life experience as an actor, it is also enriched by the laboratory of our work. I could not have written this without their loyalty, friendship, and real artistry on display week after week.

Writing is a relatively new endeavor for me, and the encouragement I've gotten from readers of my blog has meant a great deal. The many people who took the time to make interesting and constructive comments made me realize I was indeed striking a chord. Give an actor a compliment, and he will be a friend for life!

This book would never have happened without one person: Jana Branch. Jana is one of the most intelligent and incisive people I've known. She came to my acting class to inform her screenwriting, and after reading some of my early writing said, "I think you have a book here." She encouraged me, prodded me, and opened up my ideas about what this book could be. I cannot thank her enough for her guidance, unfailing efforts, and real friendship.

My own creative life would not be the same without these indelible souls: Jeffrey Tambor, who (aside from being a great friend) decisively pushed me back on the creative path when I truly needed it; John Sayles and Maggie Renzi for the enduring friendship and collaboration that I've been privileged to be a part of (and for being my true "magnetic north" in all things artistic); and, in memory, Michael Langham and Charles Nolte, who both believed in me and encouraged my work at critical points in my artistic development.

Thanks go to Jack Reuler, founder and artistic director of Mixed Blood Theatre in Minneapolis, whose vision of what the theater is, could be, and should be informed my worldview as an artist. His righteousness about people and art is infectious and steadfast. I also thank Gasper Patrico for his genuine curiosity about this endeavor, his sharp analytical mind, and his real encouragement about this chapter in my life; Bill Semans, who inspires me by remaining relentlessly creative at every age; and Charles Dennis, whose abundant creative gifts have expanded my worldview of the theater, film, and TV.

The journey wouldn't be the same without the professionalism and camaraderie of my manager Bruce Tufeld, Hector Elizondo, Haskell Wexler, Ron Perlman, Charlie Haid, Gary Ross, Debbie Zane, Marsha McManus and Atil Singh of Principal Entertainment, Bernie Carneol, Belle Zwerdling, Jillana Devine of Progressive Artists, and Kelly Garner of Pop Art Management.

And every actor needs a place to play. Thanks to the Gonda family, Barbara Witkin, and James Nisbet of the Pico Playhouse, a welcoming home for me and my students over the years.

This book found its final form because of publisher Michael Wiese, a seeker, truth-teller, and genuinely evolved thinker. Michael felt this book had a unique and different approach and took the leap along with me. I cannot thank him enough for his encouragement, wisdom, and guidance.

And last on this page but first in my heart — my wife Emily and sons Nick and Joe, whose continual love and support make so much possible. I am a husband and father who also happens to be an actor and teacher.

INTRODUCTION

Why do we act? What is the impulse? What is the process? What sustains us? When I began teaching later in life, I went back to basics. I tried to shake off years in the acting trenches, set old habits and dogma aside, and look at acting with fresh eyes.

What struck me was how individual we each are, how what we do differs so greatly from actor to actor. There are many roads to a great performance. There are many ways to live a creative life. To honor this individuality, I developed a nondogmatic approach to teaching that starts with what we all have in common and what also sets us apart — one's indelible self.

Acting is a "faith-based" profession that requires deep belief in yourself. Odds are against success, if one is to be clear-eyed about this. A life in acting takes single-minded purpose, but that purpose must also include a life outside of acting. The actor's evolving worldview, reflected back through the artist's work, is at the heart of unforgettable performances.

It's a challenge for actors to find true mentoring. The pursuit of a career in acting can be a territorial endeavor, everyone protecting whatever piece of the pie they have managed to secure. However, in this book, **I hope that you find the voice and heart of a mentor.** Whether you know yourself to be an Authentic Actor — someone who acts because the call is so strong you don't really have a choice about it — or are asking if you are, this book was written for you.

Teaching has been one of the most rewarding facets of my creative life. This book is the culmination of many years of thought, practical work in the field, and genuine curiosity about how we actors do what we do. May you find what you need here and then take it into the world.

HOW TO USE THIS BOOK

I designed this book to fit the way actors live — on the go, with unpredictable schedules. Dive in deep for an hour or dip in for 5 minutes while you wait in line at the coffee shop. Read it from start to finish, or go straight to the topics that speak to your life right now. Either way, spend time with the Explorations. That's where you will really connect with the life of an Authentic Actor.

The book has seven parts. Which are most important for you? Follow this key: ✳✳✳ = essential   ✳✳ = helpful   ✳ = optional

If you're a **beginning actor...**

1 Today's Authentic Actor	2 Who Are You?	3 What Do You Know?	4 Success Factors	5 The Audition	6 The Art of Career	7 The Business of Life
✳✳✳	✳✳✳	✳✳✳	✳✳✳	✳✳✳	✳✳✳	✳✳✳

If you're an **experienced actor** wondering about the trajectory of your career...

1 Today's Authentic Actor	2 Who Are You?	3 What Do You Know?	4 Success Factors	5 The Audition	6 The Art of Career	7 The Business of Life
✳✳✳	✳✳✳	✳✳✳	✳✳✳	✳✳✳	✳✳✳	✳✳✳

If you're a **filmmaker, writer, or other non-actor** who wants to learn how actors really think and what motivates us...

1 Today's Authentic Actor	2 Who Are You?	3 What Do You Know?	4 Success Factors	5 The Audition	6 The Art of Career	7 The Business of Life
✳✳✳	✳✳✳	✳✳✳	✳	✳✳	✳	✳

If you're **not an actor but must "perform" in front of an audience to be successful in your job** — teachers, attorneys, executives, managers, and others...

1 Today's Authentic Actor	2 Who Are You?	3 What Do You Know?	4 Success Factors	5 The Audition	6 The Art of Career	7 The Business of Life
✳	✳✳✳	✳✳	✳	✳	✳	✳

To see videos about topics in this book, go to

Michael Laskin Studio on YouTube.

https://www.youtube.com/user/MichaelLaskinStudio

To learn more about the careers and credits of people mentioned in this book, go to **IMDb (Internet Movie Database).**

www.imdb.com

1
TODAY'S AUTHENTIC ACTOR

Your "good old days" are right now.

10 EASY STEPS TO THE ACTING CAREER YOU DESERVE

1. Read this book (so far, so good).
2. Take my class.
3. Coach with me privately (payment plans available).
4. Follow my proven trademarked method (taught throughout the known universe — payment plans available).
5. Repeat steps 1 through 4.
6. Seriously! Read this book.
7. Take my 8-day Boot Camp–Intensive Immersion Experience (fasting required).
8. Don't get old.
9. Seriously! Don't get old!
10. Repeat steps 1 through 9 (financing available).

Sound familiar? We all love easy answers. We'd all like to find the magic bullet — that one thing that will put us over the top and onto the next level in our acting careers. And many people new to acting or struggling to find their way are drawn to people and methods that promise the keys to the kingdom.

In a business where there are very few true mentors for actors, there are many who make their living by trafficking in easy, ineffective answers. The myth being sold is that if you just do these things, it will all open up to you. "Our one true method is the only way to succeed." Buyer beware. The bottom line?

If it sounds too good to be true, it is.

If it feels cultish, it is.

If it feels like it's all about the money, it is.

And... if it feels *just right*, it is.

"HOW TO" ONLY GOES SO FAR

"How to" is fine as far as it goes, which isn't very far. *How to Cold Read. How to Book That Job! How to Get an Agent.* This line of thinking is a fast path to big promises that rarely deliver.

A case in point: I've worked with actors who have taken audition classes and developed a kind of skill at auditioning — but *they are not yet actors.* Their greatest fear should be actually *booking* that job and discovering the enormous difference between a slick audition and being able to do your best work at 3:00 A.M. after being on set for 14 hours. "We've got to get this shot! It's late. C'mon, let's go!"

That reality will not be found in a how-to book. When the cameras are rolling and the money meter is ticking, actors are often asked to deliver their best work under adverse conditions. The smart ones understand this, and know that there is more than booking the job. Much more.

This is not to say that you'll learn nothing from the many methods, classes, and books out there. You absolutely will — sometimes by learning what *doesn't* work. And you may meet some interesting people. (One of the best things about being in a class is the opportunity to "find your people.")

But the reality is that you can do all these how-to classes and still be basically nowhere. In fact, you can probably count on it. "How-to" is results-oriented in an endeavor that is, by definition, process-oriented. It's ass-backwards, as they say where I grew up. The actor's path is rarely clear and linear. If you ask ten artists how they found their respective ways, you will most likely find ten different, circuitous routes to what they consider success. And those ten routes were navigating an entertainment landscape that is in rapid evolution.

What do they all have in common? Craft and professionalism is their pathway to art. They mate sound career strategy and the ongoing development of one's talent with the dedication of the amateur, who works out of passion and zeal. And — most importantly — each actor understands the fingerprint that is his or hers alone and learns how to communicate it with resonance.

ASK A GOOD QUESTION

Asking a good question — rather than fixating on the search for some ultimate answer — opens up a *real* dialogue. Good questions will help you become your own guide in the scene, in your career, and in life. I believe the answer is always within, no matter what acting process you favor. We all need outside guidance, even if it points us inward in our search. And we all need to share our creative journey with a community of artists.

This isn't a how-to book. I prefer to start with basic questions I ask myself and my students again and again. Think about your own skill set:

- What do you know?
- What do you still need to learn?
- What techniques work for you every time?
- What techniques are you holding on to that don't work?

Only by asking good questions and searching within will you get past the how-to's to a deeper place. This is an ongoing process, a journey of growth in craft and artistry. If you want spoon-fed answers, the line starts over there. **If you wish to become the answer yourself — the line starts within.**

Is the actor's quest for greatness, sanity, and self-knowledge for you? If you've done all the right things, followed the right path, taken all the right classes but are still lacking something, the thing that's missing may be that which is unique to you: your fingerprint as an actor. Your authenticity — the core of your indelible self.

ARTIST? COMMODITY? OR BOTH?

I considered acting an art form long before I really thought of it as a career. Most actors think of themselves as artists. If you don't at least begin with that aspiration, I believe you are in the wrong line of work.

But here's the reality: You trained at Northwestern, Yale, USC, or NYU. You studied Meisner, Strasberg, Larry Moss (or even Michael Laskin). You've played in the gardens of Shakespeare, Chekhov, and Tracy Letts. And here you sit trying to make sense of a costar audition for a mediocre TV show you would never choose to watch. Are you just a commodity? Something to be bought and sold, exchanged in a marketplace? Your manager or agent is subtly pressuring you to book this. *C'mon... we've got to get going.*

The breakdown: That poker-faced casting director and sleepy executive are looking for a 22-year-old hunk for a crazy nightclub scene with six lines. You *are* that guy! You were amazing when you played Nick in *Who's Afraid of Virginia Woolf?* and Captain Bluntschli in *Arms and the Man.* Do they know this? Does this mean anything in the marketplace? Basically, no. It means virtually nothing to the very specific casting task on that day.

Every actor deals with a version of this dilemma:
- *Can an actor be both an artist and a commodity?*
- *Does being a commodity preclude or diminish your artistry?*
- *Can the two coexist?*
- *Does being one make you less of the other?*

This conflict is nothing new. I'm sure contemporaries of Michelangelo called him a sellout for taking on that ceiling commission. Yet those other painters would have taken that job in a heartbeat had it been offered to them.

All that being said, your talent and artistry must be important to *you* — very important, in fact. It's absolutely crucial that you hold on to these, or you will become *only* a commodity. And then your "freshness date" will quickly expire. Your task is to remain an artist for the long road ahead, whether you are 22 or 72.

At the same time, you owe it to yourself to recognize and capitalize on your core strengths as a commodity in the entertainment marketplace. One does not preclude the other. An actor may be a commodity on and off for periods of time. As they say, sometimes you're hot and sometimes you're not.

But independent of whether you are the face casting directors are looking for in a given season, you can *always* be an artist. It's what sustains you through the inevitable career ups and downs. That doesn't require affirmation in the marketplace from directors, agents, or casting directors. It only requires your time, attention, and interest — all firmly within your control.

Artist and commodity. You can be both — if you honor both.

TODAY'S AUTHENTIC ACTOR

A young student in my weekly class asked me to look at his new acting reel before he hit the marketplace with it. At 22 and fresh out of the USC School of Dramatic Arts, his work had already impressed me. But how good could his reel really be? I knew that his clips weren't from established TV shows or films. I braced myself.

He sent it to me. I watched, and I was dumbstruck. It was *very* good. Each element was fresh and dynamic. Each one showed something completely different about him as an actor. His work was excellent and memorable. In terms of production quality, every clip looked and felt like it was from an established film.

Where did all this great footage come from? He said (a bit casually), "Oh, those are from films I wrote and directed."

Bingo. This is today's Authentic Actor, firmly rooted in today's new realities.

The Authentic Actor today…
- does not ask for permission to act;
- sees his or her talent holistically, an active part of a global creative supply chain;
- doesn't wait around for the phone to ring or feel like a victim of anything;
- is propelled forward with drive, creativity, imagination, and a personal sense of storytelling;
- makes the most of limited resources and today's accessible filmmaking technology; and
- is a hyphenate: actor-writer, actor-director, actor-producer, actor–location scout, actor–craft serviceperson… but is first and foremost an actor-artist.

THE NEW CREATIVE SUPPLY CHAIN

The process of creating art on film has been democratized. Anyone with an iPhone and an imagination can create content. This does *not* mean it's any good. Much of it is dreadful. On the other hand, I believe that much of what is currently on TV and in movie theaters is pretty dreadful — just with more money.

I have a 5% rule. I believe that at any given time, in any medium (film, TV, theater), in any market (New York, L.A., London, Chicago, you name it), only 5% of what is made is really excellent. The rest is either just okay, mediocre, or simply bad.

No one deliberately sets out to create things that are bad, but nevertheless they seem to happen on a very regular basis! I encourage my students to develop the critical skills to know the difference between that 5% and the rest. If you can tell the difference, you can strive to be a part of that 5%.

Today's young actors — and older actors who want to remain relevant — are like factory workers prior to Henry Ford totally changing the way cars were made. They are like the office workers who had to learn a whole new language and morph from their IBM Selectric typewriters to computers. We are at the precipice of yet another new world, and the business (and the art that must reside inside a business structure) may be unrecognizable in five years. Don't get too comfortable, because the only constant is change.

The "good old days" are actually right now. You simply must keep your ear to the ground and your eyes on the horizon. Resist becoming mired in the past and using older modes of working or stale "been there, done that" approaches. The world will open up to you if you embrace it, so be ready.

In the 1960s, the model of the contemporary singer-songwriter emerged and fundamentally changed the contemporary music business. Bob Dylan and others took a firm grasp on writing, composing, producing, performing, and sometimes managing their art. I think actors today have the same versatility to become artists at every point within the creative chain of supply. This is a sea change and an opportunity that is new, dynamic, and exciting.

RISK AND REWARD

Acting as a creative endeavor exhilarates people. It always has, which explains why so many chase the dream. Acting as a career choice scares people. It's a huge leap from the ranks of amateur to professional, from acting because you love it to strategizing and sustaining a career. This evolution is different for everyone, but one common thread is fear.

How great is your appetite for fear, for uncertainty? Becoming fearless is part of taking life on in general, and it is an integral part of a career as an actor and artist. It tests your dedication and love for the actual work. It makes you question everything. It strains your key relationships.

Is all this worth it? Do my friends and family really understand how difficult this is on every level? Will this make me happy? **Do I really want this?**

Paradoxically, I think now may be the best time to be an artist. If you go out into the world and try to do something "safe," you may find that a lot of the so-called safe choices don't make much sense anymore in our changing world. Safe is so last century. In the 21st century, risk is the rewardable virtue.

4 LEVELS OF COMMITMENT

Over the years, I've come across four levels of commitment to the acting path. Before going any further on yours, ask yourself where you fit on this spectrum:

The Flirt: Acting might be a cool career choice. Or a whim. Flirts have one foot out the door at all times. They miss classes. They constantly reschedule key appointments. They almost never rehearse. They have a really good backup plan — which ends up becoming the real plan. They want to be able to say, "Yeah, I tried that... it just wasn't for me." As if that eventuality was their choice. They are more in love with the *idea* of it than the *doing* of it.

The Date: Some actors test out their career choice by doing something akin to dating it. They're more serious than Flirts, but they're always looking around at the party to see who else is out there, suspecting there's a better option in the next room. And guess what? They will find it, because there are so many career choices that are more logical than acting. This is usually the person who gets a degree in theater and eventually goes into public relations or advertising. There's nothing wrong with that.

The Affair: The affair is a passionate, short-term relationship that ends badly. These actors get in deep quickly, get elevated in career status early, catch a break, and get a look at the major leagues. Then at the first real disappointment, the first real test of dedication, they're out the door. You might know them as one-hit wonders. They have talent, and they got lucky. But they may have misplayed a hand or two and then didn't have enough love in their hearts, respect for their talent, or humility in the face of failure to regroup, relaunch, and try again. But their brief taste of how it could be — or might have been — stays with them for a long time.

The Marriage: The marriage is exactly that. Commitment for the long haul. A marriage is based on and fueled by love and respect. It endures the ups and downs of activity and inspiration, only to emerge reenergized, reconnected, and re-created. The marriage is a lifelong commitment. Like a marriage, a long-term commitment to being an actor takes dedication, hard work, and the continual search for innovation and reinvention. If you're up for all of that, I recommend it.

10 ESSENTIAL IDEAS FOR TODAY'S AUTHENTIC ACTOR

1. **Lead an examined life.** Be curious enough to begin to truly know who you are. Develop your own worldview. This is the beginning of understanding your personal fingerprint as an actor and an artist.

2. **Develop your talent fully, in tandem with your actor's fingerprint.** When you merge your fully developed talent with your singular identity, you become unforgettable. Dig deep and always shoot for the top. Take classes, get into plays, make short films. Learn by doing. Read history, biographies, and great fiction. See great films — including ones that were made before you were born. There's wealth out there to be discovered.

3. **Formulate an idea about what kind of actor you want to become.** Identify your acting superheroes, those whose work you admire and would like to emulate. Like those actors, stand for something and develop a point of view. Most great actors (not unlike iconic brands that resonate) have core qualities that are immediately recognizable. What does the brand of *you* stand for?

4. **Become entrepreneurial.** Talent alone is simply the "price of admission." At the professional level, everyone is talented to some extent, or they wouldn't have gotten where they are. If talent alone were the predictor of success, the stars of TV and film would be a very different group. In many cases luck is a major factor, and being entrepreneurial helps create the very luck which otherwise may prove elusive.

5. **Understand and accept this: It *is* who you know.** Develop your network of people. Who you know opens the door. Then,

bringing your fully developed talent — who you are and what you know — may get you the job. It takes all of that.

6. Understand your blink-of-an-eye factor. A wide range for an actor is a wonderful virtue, especially in the theater. But, in most cases in the worlds of film and TV, you will be called upon to play some version of yourself. Knowing yourself and having a deep sense of the core qualities you communicate becomes key. By the way, playing a version of yourself does not in any way make you less of an actor.

7. Stay connected with the world beyond acting. Acting can be an intangible pursuit. Find tangible things you can do: plant a garden, build a piece of furniture, volunteer at a food pantry. These create a connective tissue between the real world and the imagined world of an actor. Don't get lost in the "backstage" nature of the actor's life. Get lost in life. It's so much more interesting.

8. Create a strong support system of friends, family, classmates, and trusted others. The dream (and disappointments) cannot exist in a vacuum.

9. Be determined. Be optimistic. An acting career is a "faith-based" endeavor — you have to have a deep belief that you will succeed. This means staying positive. A healthy mental outlook is as important as a healthy body.

10. Enjoy yourself. Laugh often! It is play, after all.

WHAT DOES SUCCESS LOOK LIKE?

Before you can set a course for your career or life, you need to have your own idea of what success will look like. Plenty of people will have their own definitions of success for you. But only *you* know what *your* meaningful process and endpoint look like.

Many actors race to "make it" by a certain age or within a certain number of years. With youth-obsessed film and TV culture, it's easy to buy into the idea of actors, especially women, having some unspoken expiration date.

Becoming clear about how you define success will help you avoid the highs and lows that are part of any career. It will also help you make decisions that keep you on *your* track rather than getting distracted by all the peripheral "noise" in our business. And if your ideas of success are tied more to being famous than being an artist, you will perhaps pursue a different path than the one described in this book.

Write down what success looks like to you — in your career and in your life — with whatever detail comes to mind. Places to start:

What will your life look like as an actor?

What kinds of roles will you be playing?

Who will you be working with?

What skills will you have mastered?

What will your life look like when you're not acting?

What will your personal life, relationships, and home life look like?

Intention comes from clarity. And action follows intention.

2

WHO ARE YOU?

To show yourself, you have to know yourself.

IN THE BLINK OF AN EYE

When we meet someone new for the first time, we usually have a few instant impressions: shy, intelligent, warm, confident, fake, funny... We read these unconsciously from body language, dress, facial expression, tone of voice, and many other signs. We are wired to evaluate quickly, subliminally, in an instant.

This blink-of-an-eye factor is part of human business. And it's very much a part of show business. It's very important that we all understand that. It's not a negative; it just *is*.

In auditions, what I call "office acting," casting directors don't have time to discover your range. They assume you have talent; it's how you got in the room. They may glance at your credits, but in that transaction, they don't want or need to know what you can *do*. That comes later. They are more interested in *who you are*. What they're really interested in is your blink-of-an-eye factor.

That first impression answers two questions: What unique finger-print as an actor do you bring into the room? What indelible sense of self will be impressed upon their memories after you leave? **Like it or not, your indelible self and a clear worldview can sometimes trump talent and traditional acting skills.**

Excellent screen actors bring this singular sense of self to their performances — that same self that in a theater production is subli-mated into a character. They are showing us who they are, as well as what they can do. When you clearly communicate and embody your personal fingerprint, you can become unforgettable — indelible. So, **you truly need to "get" yourself before you can expect others to "get" you.** That means understanding and embracing what is unique in you — what is yours alone.

A clear sense of self can be elusive for many younger artists. Leading an examined life — always a good idea in my opinion — speeds this evolution along. As we age, we tend to become more of who we truly are. It's a natural progression, and it's a great asset for screen actors. As an older actor, for better or worse, my life is on my face.

Artists of any age, but especially younger ones, need to understand the value of that self-knowledge in their life and their art. Part of my job is to help actors jump-start that process. It isn't something that can be taught in the ordinary sense of the word. But an experienced and self-aware teacher can nurture this in younger artists, in effect inviting and guiding them onto what is a lifelong road.

YOUR PAST COMES WITH YOU

Consciously or not, everyone brings something into the room. What you think is your default position, your "neutral," is full of personality and core qualities. One of the actor's jobs is to understand what comes along.

Like it or not, your life comes into the room with you — so it's best to understand who you are and to be comfortable in your own skin. That's far easier for older actors. For younger actors, this process has to be jump-started by actively examining your life. And, in that, the line between genuine curiosity and self-obsession is always a fine one.

One of my coaching clients is the wonderful actress Camilla Luddington, of *Grey's Anatomy* and other fine credits. Camilla, aside from being lovely and very talented, has always possessed a quality of true emotional immediacy. In a visit to my weekly class, she revealed that when she was 18 she came to New York City from England, pretty much without friends or money, to pursue an acting career. Suddenly, her mother died. She went back home and, through her grief, had to ultimately decide whether she would even return to New York. Would she try to finish what she started, or stay in England because of this unexpected trauma? Camilla eventually went back to New York, determined to continue with her life, her dreams, her journey in some part as a tribute to her mother.

Camilla says that her mother's presence is always with her. It isn't overt or conscious, but she knows that she carries it into every audition room. It colors who she is. It may, in some way, explain why I have always found her to be so emotionally ready, available, and deep.

EXPLORATION

YOU, IN THE BLINK OF AN EYE

You walk into a room. Other people glance at you. What split-second impression does your presence create? For the actor, understanding even some of this is terribly important. And actors are often the worst judge of their own impact at this most basic level of human interaction.

I do this exercise with my class, and it can be very revealing. You can do this with a group of friends or fellow actors, or anyone you trust to be both perceptive and *truthful*. It's simple:

1. Have your group sit down facing your entrance.

2. Enter the room as you would if you were about to audition.

3. Make eye contact, then introduce yourself with a simple, "Hi, my name is…"

4. Each person in the room then writes down the first three words that describe you. They should go with their first instincts, without censoring their own reactions and without taking too much time to think about it.

5. Have each person say their three words out loud. Did people have consistent impressions? Are the words similar to or different from the words you would use to describe yourself?

This blink-of-an-eye impression is the tip of the iceberg for getting to know and understand your personal fingerprint as an actor.

THE IMPULSE TO ACT

Why do we act? To be clear, this is not the same as asking why we've made this extremely challenging career choice. I think if we can answer the first question, we can start to make sense of the second.

I've always thought that the impulse to act is hardwired — a basic human instinct. It's an attempt to become someone else entirely, perhaps someone grander, more heroic than ourselves. When a four-year-old puts on a fireman's hat and runs around the house putting out fires and saving lives, he's acting the way he thinks a fireman acts: brave, death-defying, important.

He's on an adventure of the imagination. And **no one had to teach him how to do this**. He knows how to do this at a blood level. When cavemen returned from the hunt, I'm sure they acted out the bravery of the kill around the fire for everyone to see and admire.

Eventually this human impulse to act became codified, and, taken to the next level, acting on the stage became the logical outlet for this transformational impulse. Theater acting is an outward gesture that, if successful, permits both you and the audience to accept the idea of you becoming someone else entirely. There's an accepted level of artifice, even in the most realistic of plays. It's fun and exciting for the actor to disappear into another person's life — their habits, walk, accent, and shoes.

However, it can also be a place to hide, serving only the needs of the character, in effect disappearing into the character. This is what most actors have been trained to do. In fact, many become actors precisely because they are more comfortable in someone else's reality than in their own. A great backstage compliment: "I didn't even see you up there. I only saw the character!"

But performers who then want to pivot from theater to working in film and TV may discover that this "hiding" behind a character can be the exact opposite of what great screen acting should be. We don't want *you* to disappear onscreen. On the contrary, we want *you* to be the identity through which the wants and needs of the character effortlessly flow.

Modern acting for the screen — film, TV, and now the Web and mobile devices — throws this hardwired concept on its ear. Screen acting is rarely the act of becoming someone else entirely. A few actors in a rarefied stratosphere are allowed to do this. Actors like Anthony Hopkins, Meryl Streep, Daniel Day-Lewis, Robert Downey, Jr., Javier Bardem, Christian Bale, and Benedict Cumberbatch are allowed to transform — and audiences marvel at the magic of this somewhat primal act precisely because it is so rare in film.

But for the most part, acting on the screen is the art of being a truthful and dynamic version of exactly who you already are, fused with a highly developed set of skills. That is the sweet spot for so many screen actors. And if you can disabuse yourself of the notion that you have to be someone else entirely, a new level of truth may take hold in your work.

REMEMBERING HOW TO PLAY

As a very broad generalization, training like the Method focuses on helping actors become more emotionally real in their work. In the first half of the 20th century, this lack of emotional realism was a hurdle for actors who grew up watching stylized performances on the screen and stage.

In the 21st century, realistic TV and film styles give us an innate understanding of what realism looks like — at least optically. Young actors have grown up with this aesthetic as the norm. Realism is a given (like software that comes preloaded on a laptop) in today's young actors. This ubiquitous realism doesn't by itself make anyone a great actor (or even a good actor). But it does create a baseline for a sense of what modern screen acting is, feels like, or could be.

What can be very foreign, however, is breaking open the actor's imagination and rediscovering the ability to play creatively. Every child understands this at a hardwired level. They instinctively know to play, to pretend, to go off on a flight of the imagination. Their truth isn't arrived at through tortuous acting exercises or substitutions or sense memory. Their truth is achieved by pure instinct.

But somewhere along the line, as we get older, we lose a connection with this instinct. We're told:

"Behave yourself."

"You're too old for that nonsense."

"Don't get into trouble."

"Grow up!"

The most interesting characters, in life and art, are the ones full of flaws and imperfections. Actors do "get in trouble." That's what we do. It's a by-product of a playful imagination that goes dormant in so many of us. Over the years we may develop a strong technique but become afraid of being silly, looking foolish, or trying and failing — which are all part of revealing ourselves fully.

FIRST INSTINCTS

Pablo Picasso famously said, "It took me four years to paint like Raphael, but a lifetime to paint like a child." At its core, acting (like Picasso's painting) is initially about having great first instincts — being able to scan a scene and quickly have a take on it that is essentially true, dynamic, and responsive. I believe that gaining an understanding of how we arrive at truth *instinctively* is the key. For me that means staying connected to the idea of play, to the imagination, to that three-year-old who didn't have to do an exercise to know the truth of a situation. That is an artist's state of mind.

That being said, all this is for naught if there is no underlying technique. Sound technique is the pathway to artistry, and there are no shortcuts in this area. You simply must put in the time to gain these skills. Take classes (you will even learn from the bad ones), act in plays, write and produce short films, say "yes" to the chance to work whenever and wherever you can as you develop your talent.

Having a solid technique guarantees that there is a level below which your work will not fall. Acting, as inspired as it may be, is (and must be) a repeatable act. If you are doing a play on Broadway, you are doing it eight times a week. If you are shooting a film, you may have to shoot a particular scene fifteen times, from different angles, making every take as fresh as the first. For the actor with little technique, the ability to appear to say something over and over again as if for the first time is a mystery. Technique is simply the framework in which the artistry resides.

THE BURDEN OF FORMAL TRAINING

Acting has changed enormously — exponentially — over the last century. But for the most part, training for the actor has not. Most schools of acting training today are still rooted in ideas brought forward in the 1930s, when New York's Group Theatre was the head-waters of new ideas about natural, emotionally charged acting. Harold Clurman, Stella Adler, Sanford Meisner, and Lee Strasberg all devised approaches that reacted to the artificial acting style that prevailed at that time. Read Harold Clurman's *The Fervent Years* to get a real history of the Group Theatre's significance.

These were seminal ideas in the 1930s, '40s and '50s. But the world has changed, audiences and delivery systems have changed, and acting has certainly changed. There is no real artificiality to rail against in today's acting landscape. There is dull acting, uninformed acting, unimaginative acting, and undisciplined acting — but realism seems to come preloaded in today's young actors. They understand it at their core. They know what it should sound like and look like. However, they often don't understand the technique, craft, artistic strategy, and imagination that fuels truthful, realistic acting.

Not that long ago, actors generally specialized in theater, film, or television. Actors were somewhat segregated — ghettoized, in fact — based on the venues they favored or that favored them. This is essentially no longer true; now nearly all actors work (or desire to work) in all areas, from stage to big screen to small screen to the very small screen of mobile devices. TV stars work on Broadway, some-times without the requisite stage chops. Meanwhile, some theater stars struggle to master the improvisatory feel of TV and film work.

The initial and obvious adjustment from stage to screen is the difference between playing to the house or playing intimately to the camera. "Make it smaller" is the mantra. But this technical difference is just the mechanics of a more fundamental adjustment that must be made. Screen acting demands that you are comfortable in your own skin, bringing all of *you* to the task with naturalistic ease. **If acting on stage is the art of successfully pretending to be someone else entirely, then the art of screen acting is to successfully be exactly who you are — mated with a highly developed set of skills.** That sounds easy, but it can be very difficult, especially for those who have been trained to pretend to be someone else. To some extent, it goes against the instincts and wiring of the four-year-old at play.

Without realizing it, actors apprentice themselves to methods that can be more of a roadblock than an open door when it comes to acting on camera. Onscreen work is a different challenge entirely. When I made the transition to acting in film and TV, my way of working — which was based on techniques learned from the most respected traditions of actor training (and had been successful on stage) — became in large part ineffective.

Both disciplines require talent, but talent is simply the price of admission. At the professional level, it is expected. What we look for in film acting — and what makes stars — is an indelible sense of self and a clear worldview.

For those who aspire to work on screen, this fundamental shift from what you can *do* to who you *are* is the source of the disconnect with theater-focused training. You can see it as a roadblock, or you can choose to see it as an opportunity.

DON'T TRANSFORM. INFORM.

The desire to act is more than something we actors simply enjoy doing. It's part of being human! We love transforming and becoming someone else entirely, disappearing into another identity. But in a very real way, film acting goes directly against that impulse. Whether you like it or not, the camera reveals *you*.

For the young actor breaking into film and television, possessing a wide range of chameleon-like acting skills (something most actors strive for) can confuse those casting decision-makers. Here's the deal: If they need someone who does an Irish accent, they'll get an Irishman — regardless of your ability to convincingly play Irish.

To be sure, there is (and has always been) a rarefied group of actors who are given the opportunity to transform on film. But the rest of us who are lucky enough to work onscreen usually play some variation of ourselves. Simply "being you" is not easy and is not the full answer to this challenge.

Consider screen legends like Jimmy Stewart, John Wayne, Audrey Hepburn, Clint Eastwood, Gene Hackman, Cary Grant, Spencer Tracy, Jack Nicholson, Robert Redford. In the seeming sameness of their performances are also potent core qualities that draw us to them, make us love them, make us root for them.

They don't transform. They inform. They offer up themselves and their worldview as the lens through which we all look. We know what they stand for. They have a singular clarifying take on the world around them that becomes the weighty center around which the rest of the story revolves. This is not a lesser form of artistry. In fact it may be a higher form, and it is uniquely cinematic.

In today's world, Brad Pitt, Leonardo DiCaprio, Tom Cruise, Sandra Bullock, and Ryan Gosling all possess strong core qualities that make them stars. Can they do anything else? Of course they can. Do they desire the transformative cachet of a Meryl Streep or a Daniel Day-Lewis? That's hard to say. Brad Pitt certainly has tried to stretch in this way, but despite his obvious talent and commitment, it's proven difficult for us to think of him anew. Can Jack Nicholson play King Lear? Probably not. But, he's the very best Jack Nicholson there is. There's no one else like him. His life and his acting have merged. He, and others like him, inform us not by transforming but by being deeply personal.

That's why Seth Rogen, for instance, probably wouldn't be a very good Hamlet — but he's the best imperfect, odd, funny Seth Rogen there is. He has a worldview that we, as the audience, know in the blink of an eye. That worldview is revealed because he has no artifice. He is completely comfortable with his persona being the lens through which we see a story unfolding. He has a definite lack of traditional theater-based actor skills. He is an extreme example of an indelible sense of self triumphing over traditional skills. He makes it look easier than it is in reality. He faces the same obstacles we all do when working. He just doesn't have the added burden of thinking he needs to be anyone else.

THE CAMERA AND THE METAPHYSICAL YOU

The art and pursuit of truth in acting is endless. We can find it in an office in front of a casting director on the Sony lot at 4:30 P.M. We can find it on location in front of a camera lens — a lens that sees right into us. We can also find it onstage every night in a live performance. But in film and TV, the camera finds and reveals moments beyond our conscious awareness. That's the you that is more than physical. **Our relationship to the camera is sometimes metaphysical.**

I profoundly experienced this sensation working with a young Johnny Depp on the original *21 Jump Street*, a TV series on which I portrayed the mayor of the fictitious city where these young cops worked. On the first day we shot our scenes, I saw nothing out of the ordinary. However, when I watched it on TV, I was blown away, catching nuances in Johnny's work that I simply did not notice face-to-face. The camera revealed the scene quite differently than my perception of it in real time. That's when I knew he possessed a unique gift.

They say perception is reality, but I learned that this is not necessarily true when the camera and an actor like Johnny Depp are involved. The camera simply revealed him. He didn't do much, and he didn't have to. Johnny had something special, he knew it, and he had the good sense to really work at becoming an artist — mating the magic he naturally possessed in front of the camera with real skill. He has a metaphysical relationship with the camera; he communicates beyond what the human eye sees in real time. Another way to put it: The camera loves him.

As actors, we plan and strategize as we prepare our work, but the camera ends up revealing other things we did not plan — things outside of our perception. That's the magic, that's the fun, that's the terror, and that's what makes film acting at its very best so wonderful and surprising.

Once you can get your head around the fact that you don't necessarily have to be anyone else, the process of acting opens up. A forgotten line or a prop out of place — an "accident" becomes an opportunity that can make film work more dynamic, more in the moment. Imperfection is what interests us and draws us in. **The human condition can be illuminated with merely a thought on camera, a shadow of emotion playing across the face.**

Combine this with a creative strategy for a scene, and you will be open to seizing accidents as interesting detours. When we can see the pores of your skin on screen, we can also read your soul, your heart, your life force — all in the blink of an eye. If you let us.

YOU ARE THE ANSWER

As an actor, your greatest renewable resource, your constant inspiration, and your deep well of strength are looking at you in the mirror every morning. Like it or not, you are the answer. And that answer is found within. It's you. It's you that they want — the real you, not the one hiding in the character's costume or in acting class. Only you can put in the work and possess the desire to reveal yourself in ways that are unforgettable. Only you can illuminate a character like no one else.

That's your personal fingerprint as an actor and artist — the core of your indelible self. And that's ultimately the only thing that truly separates you from everyone else. The other actors hanging around waiting to audition may be talented as well, but they are not you.

Once you give up the notion that you have to be somebody else, everything will start to get easier. That burden is released, because *you* are enough — as long as it's a real, fully examined you. So who are you?

WHAT'S "WRONG" WITH YOU IS STILL YOU

RJ Mitte, the young Walter White, Jr. in the acclaimed TV series *Breaking Bad*, was born with a mild cerebral palsy that was used to great effect in the show. I occasionally coached RJ, but never on finding the emotion in a scene. Ever. The emotional part of any scene is easy for him. His only real performance issue was the occasional difficulty enunciating words, a remnant of speech issues related to his condition.

His life is on his face, in his walk, in his laugh and his eyes, and out there for all to see. His emotional intelligence is extraordinarily high owing to, in no small part, the challenges faced in his real life. Through his emotional clarity, our work was a case of the student teaching the teacher!

We all have a narrative for our lives that usually includes a few thoughts that fall under the heading "What's wrong with me?" It's a narrative that can either help or hurt us. What's that voice in your head saying? Do any of these sound familiar?

- *I'm not pretty / handsome enough.*
- *I'm too pretty / handsome — they don't take my talent seriously.*
- *I don't look right.*
- *No one "gets" me.*
- *I'm too old.*

An obsession with what we hold as most desirable — even perfection — can really undermine one's confidence and self-image. Truth is messy. We're all a little (or a lot) messy. Anyone who says otherwise isn't telling the truth. Those edges are what make us particular and memorable. Rounding them off so you look more like the latest Hollywood type just makes you less of yourself. You become more of a commodity and less of an artist. Perfection can be boring. Don't try to fit the mold. Make the mold fit you.

"Make them like the face you've got..."

— RUTH GORDON, actress / writer

WHAT GETS IN YOUR WAY?

Over the years, I've come across a few standard archetypes among young actors. These archetypes all have strategies that, on the surface, can look like strengths. But watch the career trajectory (usually short) of these actors, and this "strength" becomes the weakness that prevents them from moving forward creatively, artistically, and professionally.

The truth? These archetypes are masks for fear. Do any of these sound familiar?

The Perfectionist says, "That was almost right. One more take. Just one more take, and I'll be perfect..."

The A Student says, "I memorized the lines and hit my marks. I even got there early. Why didn't I get the job?"

The Control Freak says, "How can anyone expect me to do great work in a room that is this cold / hot / crowded / stuffy...?"

The Know-It-All says, "Um, I hear you, but I have a better idea. Trust me. I know the best way to do this."

The Egotist, aka Celebrity In His / Her Own Mind aka Famous-In-Waiting says, "If those idiots would just open their eyes to my genius..."

The Strategist says, "If I go on X auditions over the next X weeks, statistically I should get X callbacks, and within X months I should have X offers..."

The Free Spirit says, "I was so *on* yesterday, but my audition is today, and I just don't feel inspired. I might just go to the beach."

EXPLORATION

YOUR LIFE NARRATIVE

What's your life narrative? What's your "story"? What events have shaped you? What experiences define who you are? Make a list of the key events in your personal life, emotional and physical. Don't overthink it. There are no right or wrong answers. Write them down, then read them over. Be honest with yourself and ask:

- Are there parts of my story that are holding me back?

- Are there events I see as limitations that can be strengths?

- Do my obvious strengths represent the real me, or do they sometimes stand in the way?

- What am I afraid of?

- Am I motivated by what I want, or am I trying to please others?

Your story is all part of what makes you uniquely you. Warts and all, it defines you. The act of writing it down is an opening to clarity. The sooner you understand it, the sooner you can manage it and make it work to your advantage.

SEEKING AND REACHING FOR GREATNESS

Witnessing greatness does not make you great. Only by *experiencing* greatness can you truly have your own barometer for it. At the end of the day, real talent is real, funny is funny, great is great, and the rest sorts itself out.

In my own career, no matter how elastic artistic standards are on any particular job, I will always have my "Michael Langham barometer." Artistic director of the Guthrie Theater from 1971 to 1977, Langham spoiled me for other directors. No one since has ever quite measured up. Perhaps it was because I was 27, and I was willing to give my acting self over to him. You had to. He was autocratic, and many thought him difficult.

To be honest, Michael made most of your acting decisions for you, whether you realized it or not. As a director, he created the world you inhabited so completely that your decisions were inevitable. He was not above giving you a line reading. Many actors bristled under these constraints, but I gave myself over to him because I had seen his incandescent productions and said to myself, "I want to be a part of *that.*"

Michael was a general leading you into battle, and I was more than happy to be a good soldier. I wanted to be part of something larger than myself — which is part of what greatness embodies.

Seek out those you identify as possessing greatness, and don't worry about their feet of clay. They are human, after all, so don't expect them to be saints. Attend their lectures, see their movies, go to their plays, listen to their music, and study their paintings. Find a way to work with them. Get as close to that flame as you possibly can. It will make you better at everything you do.

ARTISTIC SUPERHEROES

The concept of superheroes goes all the way back to Greek mythology and has always occupied a place in the human imagination. And when summer movie season rolls around, let's face it: Superheroes rule.

As actors, most of us will never know the unique challenge of bulking up and slaying the enemy in front of a green screen. But some very fine actors have donned superhero garb and somehow come out of it unscathed: Jeff Bridges, Stanley Tucci, Tim Roth, Nick Nolte, Natalie Portman, Sam Rockwell, Ian McKellen... It is possible to be a great actor *and* a superhero.

As artists battling the evil forces that push careers to the commodity end of the artist-commodity spectrum, we truly need artistic superheroes. We need to keep our eyes on those whose integrity, innovation, standards, and bodies of work elevate them to this status, and who inspire us to be better.

Your artistic superhero might be your high-school drama teacher, a college professor, or an acting teacher who helped you break through to the next level. It might be fellow actors, writers, and directors whose work has inspired you, who pushed you to reach higher.

Artistic heroes can be found in any discipline. Being a classic-jazz fan, I deeply admire Louis Armstrong for his music, life, innovative artistry, and ultimately his deeply affecting humility. From any discipline or era, people have struggled and triumphed in creative lives that can inspire your own.

Seek out the wisdom, knowledge, and challenges of artists on whose shoulders you stand. Don't fall prey to the blindness I see in many young artists, who don't know anything that happened before they were born. I find it beautiful that there are still great films I have yet to see, books I have yet to read, recordings I have yet to hear. Our creative inheritance is endless. Do yourself a favor and get lost in it.

FOLLOW YOUR ARTISTIC SUPERHEROES

Which artists inspire you to set your standards high and always shoot for the top? They may be actors, writers, directors, painters, singers, composers, or artists from other disciplines. Who motivates you? Who represents the pinnacle of achievement you would like to reach?

Make a list. Put their pictures and words on your mirror as reminders. Study their work. See where this takes you. Let them inspire you to go out and do as well — or even better.

3

WHAT DO YOU KNOW?

Excellence is on the other side of comfort.

THE AMATEUR IN THE PROFESSIONAL

I believe that the foundation of acting is craft. Picasso learned to paint classically before he spent the rest of his life learning to paint like a child. He had the underpinnings of solid craft and technique. **Great craft and technique (achieved only through hard work and time well spent) are the portals to artistry.** You've got to earn your artistry by laying the foundation with thought, diligence, and care. In this there are no shortcuts.

In modern parlance the word "amateur" describes someone who is unprofessional or unskilled at something. But remember that the meaning of the Latin *amatore* (from which *amateur* is derived) literally means to be a "lover of." So to be a real amateur, in the original sense of the word, is to be a lover of something — a lover of a pursuit, perhaps. I believe that the best professionals perform with the heart of an amateur.

PROCESS IS THE THING

The Walt Disney Concert Hall in Los Angeles is a beautiful venue, but getting to it from Studio City can be a bear in traffic. As experienced Angelenos, my wife and I left home early so we'd be sure to arrive in time for a performance of the L.A. Philharmonic. Bad traffic miraculously did not materialize, and we ended up arriving 30 minutes early.

We took our seats. Soon after, a violinist came onstage and began to warm up. We recognized him as an older Russian gentleman who'd played with the L.A. Phil for more than 30 years. He was the only figure on stage for about ten minutes. Eventually, other orchestra members slowly wandered in to fill the hall with that unique cacophony of brass, woodwinds, strings, and timpani tuning up and warming up, a sound heard only before orchestral concerts.

But that violinist, who has played for some 50 years and performed all over the world, was first on stage. I was struck by his dedication, discipline, and sense of purpose. And I was moved by his beginning anew, doing what was required to perform up to the standards he had set for himself. His process was transparent — and fascinating. I watched as he ran scales, played small snippets of melodies, and often paused in thought before he launched the next creative thrust, meditatively repeating the preparatory techniques he had honed over a lifetime. His craft, artistic habits, and love of what he does were on full exhibition. It was a performance he didn't realize he was giving, but I saw it clearly and carry its lessons with me.

An actor's audience sees only the result but rarely (if ever) the live process — what takes place in the privacy of rehearsal rooms and movie location trailers, and on stages. The audience isn't privy to our missteps along the way, except in behind-the-scenes featurettes, blooper reels, and end credits that show botched takes or stars forgetting their lines. People love to see the process, no matter how messy. In fact, the messier the better.

For the most part, actors' processes remain hidden, sometimes even from themselves. We screen actors often prepare in private (sometimes in a vacuum), and then present the results publicly — always striving for our preparation to be seamless and invisible. Maybe that's why seeing the violinist, for ten minutes of what I'm sure were countless hours of practice in private, was methodical, transparent, and calm. **As actors, we can get caught up in our results-oriented pursuits, becoming so focused on the outcome that we lose sight of the fact that the process is, in fact, the road map to the result.**

The violinist humbly revealed a bit of his process, and the opportunity to watch him prepare was quite intimate. Despite the fact that he was onstage in a major concert hall, he was alone in his preparation even though his private efforts were in full view. He could have just as easily been in his living room, wearing his slippers. As I watched my Russian friend patiently go through his paces, I was moved.

ARTISTIC STANDARDS

For a concert violinist, skill is absolute and verifiable. There are accepted standards for what a violinist does. There is no middle ground, really. He can play the Brahms violin concerto as it should be played, or he can't. Above and beyond that, one can discuss artistic merits. But technically, certain accepted benchmarks must be met. Without that, there is no art possible in his world.

Acting doesn't have that kind of verifiable standard. For actors, there rarely is a technical benchmark that must be met, unless you're dealing with Shakespeare, Shaw, or Molière. So what constitutes a good-to-great performance is far more subjective, opinions being the currency of directors, audiences, critics, and teachers.

But becoming truly great still requires that dedication and humility I saw our Russian violinist display on the stage prior to a performance by the L.A. Philharmonic. Even after 30 years in the orchestra, alone on the stage warming up, he played as an "amateur" in the true sense of the word — *a lover of.* Allowing the few of us in our seats early to observe his preparation gave a humanity to his art above and beyond the concert performance to come.

He made it all look effortless — the ultimate sign of great technique — like Fred Astaire dancing, appearing brilliantly and stylishly weightless. But I sure would have loved to watch Astaire rehearse, to work out his problems, find his way, figure things out. I would have loved to see him sweat — literally. His effortless artistry was the result of talent, yes, but it was developed and strengthened through a process driven by love of his art. His highly refined technique transcended mere skill to become art.

EXPLORATION

THIS IS WHAT I KNOW

I ask every new student in my classes to do this exploration. They prepare it at home, then read it out loud to the class (no memorization required). By talking about what you know, you reveal a sense of who you are — how you think, what you value, what makes you laugh, and more. In short, I want to know... what you know.

Feel free to do it for yourself and read it out loud to a fellow actor or other truthful advisor. Here's how:

Start with an empty pad of paper (or blank screen, if you're the typing sort) and write a series of sentences starting with "This is what I know..." There's no limit on length or scope. Most people fill a few to a dozen pages.

Be thoughtful, but don't get bogged down. Just write what's on the top of your mind as you look around your world. Honesty, stream of consciousness, and random thoughts are more useful than worrying about good grammar (and there are no grades anyway).

Your thoughts may range from mundane to deep. To get going, start with what's around you: "I know I like my coffee first thing right after I get up" or "I know I hate L.A. traffic."

You might write about things that resonate emotionally: parents, siblings, expectations, children, failure, fear, love, and so on. What parts of your background, current beliefs, priorities, and emotional truths are critical to this path you've chosen?

This isn't meant to be therapy. There's no need to confess your deepest, darkest secrets. But you do need to gain an understanding of your worldview. It's a significant element of you becoming an Authentic Actor.

DISCOVER WHAT WORKS FOR *YOU*

Every actor with some degree of experience walks into the room with a set of skills — basic tools of the acting trade. These are all the technical, physical, and emotional things you know how to do. Memorize lines. Break down a scene. Use your body and voice effectively. Create a fully formed character.

Actors acquire these skills in any number of ways, formally and informally. We learn in classes, in plays, in workshops. We learn in our BFA programs and in community theaters. We learn from that one inspired high-school drama teacher who had a passion that was infectious. We learn from having the privilege of watching people who are masters do their work, and we learn from each other. We learn on the set, and we learn simply by playing as we did when we were children, trying out new things. Sometimes (once in a while) we even learn from books.

I'm agnostic when it comes to "schools" of training for actors. I don't believe there is, ever has been, or ever will be one true method or technique in the training of actors. How could there be for an art and craft whose boundaries and parameters are constantly in flux? How can there be one true method given the huge variety in learning styles and each actor's particular needs?

All methodologies can lead to truth. The point is getting there and, along the way, discovering a working method that organically fits you. The real constants in the world of acting are continual change and evolution; an actor can only maintain his or her personal connection to the work and to revealing the truth of the scene.

"There's no rhyme or reason to this business. The best actors don't get the best roles. The best shows don't get on the air. So that's why you have to love what you do."

— MARK PIZNARSKI, director / producer / writer

FEAR OF FAILURE, FEAR OF SUCCESS

Fear of failure and fear of success are two sides of the same coin. Most of the time young actors who come for class or coaching are serious-minded and truly want to challenge themselves to learn, improve, and become more of what they know in their hearts they can be. But once in a while, an actor will come in with an attitude that this "acting thing" is something to try on for size. Not a passion. Not a drive. Not a need. Try it, and if it doesn't pan out, "that's cool."

I've seen this kind of casual attitude before, and far from being genuinely blasé, this sort of take-it-or-leave-it flirtation masks a very real fear of failure. *The hard slap in the face is that acting will leave you well before you get the chance to leave it.* No risk, no reward. No failure... no success.

Conversely, the fear of success can also be crippling. It's fear of the unknown, with perhaps some sense of your own unworthiness thrown in. We sometimes get used to failure. Failure is reliable. Failure is a place to hide out. People often get used to a prescribed life and crave order. Success, especially sudden success, can truly make your life chaotic for a time. It can upset the balance of things. It can also create a space in your life from which you can fail all over again.

But unless we're pushing our own limits, we're not learning. This involves what I call failing forward. Sometimes we have to lose our way in order to honestly discover something that touches a deeper truth in a role and in ourselves. **The only real failure is not to put in the effort.**

STINK UP THE JOINT!

I firmly believe that failure is one of the building blocks of success. If we're not pushing our boundaries, we're not learning. If we're not learning, we're stagnating. I tell my students that I'd rather they *stink up the joint* than play it safe. Class is a place to explore, a safe place to fail: the process of discovering what doesn't work on the way to finding what does.

I'm a firm believer in what I call constructive failure. Failing to learn your lines or show up on time (for example) aren't what we're talking about here; craft is essential. Your art will take flight or flop, guided by the freedom and discovery of that inner four-year-old's sense of imagination and play. But if you're afraid to look like a fool, your progress becomes incrementalized, safe, and dull. Failure is one step down, two steps up.

It's wasted effort to worry about whether you're doing great or failing, just as it's a waste of energy to beat yourself up or get mad about a past performance. Turn that energy into motivation. Learn from it. Take a lesson from failure that propels you forward.

Excellence is on the other side of comfort. You have to hold yourself to your own standards, because the reality of this business is that you will be asked to stand in line for mediocrity.

START WITH THE TEXT

The actor's artistic strategy can be quite different between stage and screen. In the theater you are playing a two-hour story and character arc every night from beginning to middle to end. Aside from figuring out beats and moments, it also requires a macro approach, the ability to look at the whole thing from 10,000 feet and see how you fit into the larger picture. It is an actor's medium. The actors drive the play forward every night.

Theater is one of the last "handmade" arts. No two performances are ever the same. The repetition from night to night is always open to little creative deviations. In the theater there is room for the actor to play and experiment, all in an effort to get to larger and deeper truths, extract two laughs in a moment where previously there was only one, or earn a moment of effective silence. On stage, actors respond and react to each other, the audience, and — when it really clicks — the universe at large. That's when a cast becomes a cohesive ensemble.

In film you do not play the whole story arc every night in a linear, beginning-to-end fashion. You play small moments of the whole story out of sequence, each scene having its own small arc that exists as a part of the larger whole. This is a medium for directors and editors to the extent that they control the pace and rhythm of the final product. All you can do as an actor is try to keep the whole story somewhere in your head and play the small human moments that all add up to the whole.

So the strategies are quite different, but there is a common starting point: the text. Start, but don't stop, with the text. This is key with any script, stage or screen. Looking for the operative word in a sentence or discovering different meanings in a repeated word or phrase can lead to moments of truth.

In TV and film — as many screenwriters painfully learn — the text (unlike in theater, where legally not a word can be changed) is not sacred. And frankly, in TV and film some of the writing can be flat, dull, obvious, or merely expository. No matter. The actor still must look for opportunities to make the scene more than what it is on the page.

Sometimes our work is "down the middle of the page," and sometimes our work is in the margins. In fact, our job is giving life to words — life that is real, true, surprising, and dynamic. This starts — always — with the text.

ROAD MAP OF A SCENE

Creating a strategy for a scene — a road map — is the way to get beyond the mechanics and into the emotional life of what's happening. Actors have different ways of going about this, but I always start with a few basic questions:

What just happened? Everyone who enters a room, in life or in the movies, comes from somewhere. Something happened just minutes or hours ago that colors that person's attitude, openness, sense of humor, physical demeanor... The life of the scene starts with its pre-life.

What's about to happen? Who and what are driving the scene? Giving away too much too soon is a typical mistake actors make. When an actor enters "loaded" for a scene, it can kill the anticipation the audience is experiencing. As viewers, we know where we're headed too soon. We crave the journey, not the arrival.

Even when a scene is predictable, search for a way to make it your own — to make the journey we know we are about to take unique. If you've heard the blues, you understand very quickly the somewhat simple musical structure. It's predictable in its form. The difference is how an artist like B. B. King would play it as opposed to how one like Buddy Guy would. The form is the same; the journey is not.

The journey is personal to each artist. I've heard "Rhapsody in Blue" dozens of times over the years. I know the melody well, and I know the turns in mood and tempo. But when a different artist plays it, the song changes. And when it's played with passion and personality, it becomes new again.

What does my character want in this scene? What's preventing me from getting what I want? What are the stakes? Making strong decisions about a character's aims and obstacles is the difference between a nice, general scene and a sparkling, specific scene. If those needs and wants aren't evident in the script, the actor must find them by discovering the meaning of what his character is *not* saying or doing.

Establishing your character's point of view in a scene is very often about the silences, the moments of slight indecision. What you are choosing not to say or do is often key to propelling what your words and actions are beyond the surface of the script.

Pretend that what's happening is happening to you. How would you react? Then, how would your character react? How far is the distance between you and your character? Understanding that distance informs the road map that makes a scene dynamic and compelling.

Where and when does the scene change? Who has the power in the scene? I think of scenes like music. There's a rhythm, and the changes (beats or new tempos) give scenes the dynamic interest that keep the audience moving forward with you. We respond to rhythms in music, in conversation, in silences. Think of your scene as an aria in an opera. What is the high note? Why? Understanding where the scene changes illuminates the arc of the scene from beginning to end. If you know where you're headed, you know better where to begin. And you know the journey of the scene in greater depth.

Is there silence in the scene? If so, where? And why? Silence is intimately related to listening. Letting a line land on you and letting emotion register can leave an important space for the audience to fill in. Leave room in your acting for the audience or your scene partner to fill in some emotional content. Simply stop, when it makes sense, and don't continue until the next thought or impulse propels you forward.

Leaving space in a scene has to be a conscious choice. Otherwise, we power through to the end without creating room for others to be a part of the journey. The great Count Basie was as famous for the notes he didn't play as he was for the ones he did play. He left large open spaces within songs that, once the music was moving forward, the audience was happy to fill in with their imaginations.

CRYING ON THE TWENTIETH TAKE

Crying on command is a talent some actors have and some don't. Actors with theater-based training may want to get themselves deeply into an emotional moment to produce the required waterworks. That works for a single performance a night. But what about on a film or TV set, take after take?

Try this at home. Decide to cry. That's it. Simply decide to arbitrarily cry — no emotional preparation necessary at all. Just dive in. Devote a full 30 seconds to this — nothing less. Do some heavy-duty crying. Get out of breath, make your shoulders heave, wipe your nose. After a full 30 seconds of this, stop and take stock: Your face will be flushed, you may be out of breath, your eyes have possibly started to wet, and your nose will be moist.

This is advice you won't find in any other acting book: Fake it! But then notice how the action of *pretending* to cry triggers those physical responses in your body that can open the portals to the real emotions behind crying. Emotions live in the body as well as the mind, and pretending to cry (or laugh) can summon muscle memory.

Is this a cheap trick? No. Is this a legitimate way into an emotional moment? Absolutely. Is it the only way? Of course not, but it is one way that proves that you don't always have to feel everything down to the deepest fiber of your soul — a viable option to have on the twentieth take.

VISUAL LITERACY

A young student of mine had difficulty starting scenes. He seemed unable to explode into a scene when it was called for. He was indecisive, afraid of making a wrong move. He needed a dose of James Cagney, perhaps the most decisive actor ever. Cagney just planted his feet, looked people straight in the eye, and said his lines with a distinctive swagger.

I advised my student to watch a James Cagney movie. Blank stare. The subtitle would have read, "Who's James Cagney?" After some back and forth, I realized that he knew almost nothing about films that were made before he was born. James Cagney was more than a half-century removed from his vantage point.

I asked other students and discovered that almost no one in my class knew the work of a pantheon of great U.S. actors: Cagney, Humphrey Bogart, Spencer Tracy, Bette Davis, Cary Grant, Kate Hepburn, Jimmy Stewart, Steve McQueen, Jane Fonda, George C. Scott, Gene Hackman, Robert Duvall, and so many more.

I refer to this affliction as visual illiteracy. If you were training to be a painter, you would never think of not knowing the work of Renoir, Miro, Picasso, Rembrandt, or Rothko. Why should acting be any different? **We stand on the shoulders of those who came before us.** We need to know the great Billy Wilder films and those of Stanley Kubrick, William Wyler, and on and on. This, too, is part of your training, and with 24/7 access to nearly all the great films ever made, there is no excuse not to be visually literate.

The story has a happy ending. He watched *White Heat* and came back the next week wide-eyed with wonder at the film and Cagney's performance. There is an almost endless amount of filmic treasure readily available to those who seek it out. Deep dive into film history, and you will be rewarded richly. Some of it may seem old-fashioned and dated, of course. But there is also magic to be discovered and savored.

The films in "AFI's 100 Years... 100 Movies" are a great beginning. Find the list online at www.afi.com.

THOUGHTS ON ACTING-CLASS CULTURE

I've never much liked acting classes. When I was asked to start one of my own, I decided to make it the kind of class I would want to attend.

I have very clear opinions and prejudices about this, arrived at through years of experience. This is how I see it, with no apologies. I always offer prospective students, whether they end up studying with me or not, two pieces of advice:

Study acting with an actor. This sounds rather basic, but there are many non-actors teaching the craft. You certainly can learn other useful things from non-actors, but they have not been in your shoes. So study with an actor who has walked into those rooms and killed. Study with an actor who understands your self-doubt, your talent, and your challenges. Study with someone who has a track record across many media (feature films, shorts, television, theater, online series). Study with someone who is a practitioner engaged in the discipline, profession, and way of life. In short: *Study with someone who has lived this life and succeeded at it.*

Do not study with those who need to be worshipped. The class should be about you, not the teacher. No gurus, please. Because at the end of the day, you have to find your own way.

Bottom line: Most of us, if we possess any talent at all, already know how to do this at some hardwired level. What we need is some sound strategy, an ongoing artistic challenge, and a place to creatively breathe. We need to be reminded of our talent, our joy, our imagination, our confidence... ourselves. We can easily get stalled or sidetracked by bad training, one-size-fits-all methodology, and teachers who need to be adored.

Classes can be great as a place to breathe oxygen into our creative lives. At certain points, they are essential. A sense of community is one key aspect of this, above and beyond artistic development. Sharing resources, discoveries, encouragement, and failures is all part of learning to define success that emanates from your truth, personal and professional. A group of likeminded actors exploring together can support you in your quest to become a more dynamic and truthful version of who you already are (and are becoming).

MOTIVATION FROM MEDIOCRITY

The notion that you learn as much or more from failure as from success, like most clichés, contains a grain of truth. Adversity, failure, shame, and loss of pride are all great motivators. What doesn't kill you makes you stronger.

When I first came to Los Angeles, I had ten years of making my living as a professional actor, primarily onstage. I had years during which I worked 40 to 45 weeks onstage, eight shows a week. One develops a high level of skill and polish in this crucible.

I came to L.A. in the fall of 1983, having just concluded a run of a play off-Broadway, following success with it in Los Angeles and London. I was 32 and had been onstage continuously since I was 18. Within a month I landed a good agent, and within six weeks I landed my very first TV job — a guest-star role on a one-hour TV series. I thought: *This Hollywood thing is easy!*

The show was formulaic, superficial TV fare, and my part was simply one of those cog-in-the-wheel roles that advances the plot. My three days of shooting were uneventful. Being new to TV shooting, I was frustrated by the waiting around, the complete lack of rehearsal, a director who was happy to get any version of the shot and move on, and the complete absence of any artistic mission. This absolutely was show "business," and it felt cold and foreign.

Within six weeks of shooting, I'd notified all my family members (and friends) that my TV debut was imminent. They were all watching, as was my wife and myself in our very cool, old Los Feliz apartment. The excitement built, the show was unfolding, and, all of a sudden, there I was. I watched intently. When it was over I sat in sullen silence. As a professional, I was embarrassed.

Was this the guy who had just starred off Broadway? Was this the same actor from the Guthrie Theater, an award winner at the Edinburgh Festival? The guy who had just done a brilliant job in the Canadian premiere of *Talley's Folly*? Was this what the major uprooting of my life and moving West was all about?

My performance was flat, false... mediocre. I was humbled and realized I had a lot to learn about being truthful on film. I never wanted to feel that way about my work again.

It forced me to look at everything I thought I knew in a new way and discard what wasn't working. And it ultimately freed me from a level of artifice in my work and allowed me to be at ease with the camera coming toward me.

CRUCIBLE EXPERIENCES

Sometimes in acting we are thrown into the fire, and we have to survive. These crucible moments are what shape us and make us stronger. When I was an actor with the Guthrie Theater, we routinely understudied several parts since we were doing true rotating repertory — a different play every night. We also were, in those days at least, never rehearsed for the roles we understudied. We were simply expected to know them.

One part I understudied was in the play *La Ronde*. When you have eight roles to cover and haven't rehearsed any of them, you tend to focus more on roles played by actors who might be older, maybe those who drink or are diabetic. It's more likely that you'll have to go on at some point for that kind of actor.

The part I understudied in *La Ronde* was played by a young, strong, and reliable actor — the picture of health! I didn't spend much time learning that role since I had seven others to learn. He was the one who broke his leg. Not only did I not really know the role, I wasn't even in that production and had not been in any rehearsals. I'd only seen it once!

I had 36 hours to learn two very long scenes — 40 pages of dialogue total — before going onstage in front of paying customers who expected a very high level of excellence. I killed myself for 36 hours. No sleep and with only the guidance of the play's director, Ken Ruta. Without his help, I could have never done it.

I miraculously learned the lines, learned the blocking, went on, and was actually quite good in the role (I was told… I have no memory of it, kind of like a war experience). The impossible had been achieved. People were frankly stunned that I was able to do it, as was I. It took me two weeks to physically recover from the effort.

But the lesson learned was that **I could do far more than I thought I could**. From that moment on, from that crucible experience, I never doubted my ability to focus, learn, and make something happen — very quickly if need be. It shaped me. It almost killed me, but it also made me tougher. The terror of moments like these, if you are lucky enough to experience them, takes you to an entirely new level in your sense of what is possible.

SOMETIMES IT'S SIMPLE

When I started teaching, one of the first people to sign up was a friend, Joanna Rubiner, someone who'd always impressed me as being very smart, funny, and highly imaginative. Professionally, she identified as a voice actor and a writer, so I was surprised when she signed up — and I think she was, too! She had always shied away from acting on stage or screen, preferring the anonymity of voiceover work.

As the class evolved, I realized that Joanna's totally unique sense of self was not going to fit any mold. She had the personality and will to make the mold fit her. She wasn't formally trained as an actor, so she had no idea of how it was "supposed to go." She just went at her scene work with complete abandon, producing rather amazing and memorable results.

One night in class, after she'd done a particularly powerful scene, I observed, "I know you're not trained in acting, but you're creating interesting, well-informed results. I'm curious — how do you approach a scene? What do you think about? Do you have some method you can articulate?"

"Well" — she thought for a minute — "I just pretend that what's happening is happening to me."

After my somewhat rambling question, the simplicity of her answer hit me right between the eyes. Brilliant, Joanna. When an actor is evolved, imaginative, curious, and unburdened by theatrical dogma and acting class B.S., the answer is simple. And smart.

I pretend that what's happening is happening to me.

We can all go home now.

THINKING ON FILM

We often don't realize how much we communicate by doing very little. To explore this, create a silent 30-second narrative in your head. You can include one physical gesture if you wish, but no words.

Film yourself in close-up thinking through your story. Show the film to other people. Do they see a story similar to what you were thinking? My students have filmed "thinking" stories such as:

My girlfriend / boyfriend just left me.

Someone I find really attractive just flirted with me.

I just found out I landed the role.

I just read a book that changed my life.

My dad just went into rehab — again.

My roommate moved out without paying the rent.

4

SUCCESS FACTORS

We're all long shots.

TALENT, INSTINCT, AND STRATEGY

Acting is a basic human instinct. Most acting training decodes what you are already doing instinctively (if you have any innate talent or imagination), gives it a name or a label, makes you conscious of it, and in doing so sometimes messes with what is a clean, organic process.

This is not to say that actor training isn't useful. It often is. It provides you a platform on which to experiment; it gives you an opportunity to put in the requisite hours to see a path to real achievement; and it even provides "oppositional learners" a point of view they can resist. But good training should create as few roadblocks as possible, leaving a clear path between your instincts and your resulting truth.

No one can teach talent. Talent is, at its most basic level, having great first instincts. If you gave an interesting scene with real conflict, strong writing, and the element of surprise to 100 random non-actors, only a few of them could look at it for just a few minutes and come up with a dynamic first take on how to play that scene. Those are the people who possess talent at its most basic level. If you cannot do that, then I believe you do not possess a talent for acting. You may have many other wonderful talents, but acting is not among them.

First instincts. The rest is strategy — which is *very* important. **Talent without strategy is the difference between a wish and a plan.** If you're reading this, you're probably someone who has the talent but may not yet have a strategy for the work, the career, the life.

TALENT IS JUST THE PRICE OF ADMISSION

How important is talent to the actor? It's the price of admission. Without it, you haven't much of a chance. With it, you've gotten through the first door.

Developing actors often obsess about whether they have any talent. Once that question gets answered — and it will be — through plays, classes, short films, hard work, and self-examination, the looming abyss of "what's next?" appears.

Very soon you'll find that at a certain level in the profession, nearly everyone has some degree of talent or they wouldn't have made it into the right rooms. So talent is assumed. It's a given. There are many other factors that then become equally, if not more, important than talent.

Now, to be sure, there are those actors who go on the long list I call "lucky people in show business," but that doesn't mean they're without talent. It may simply mean that their talent has been rewarded in a way that is out of proportion to its size.

It's imperative that talent be developed, honed, nurtured, and exercised. That is every artist's responsibility. And as you get older in this pursuit, you lose the fear of the younger actor that the talent will disappear if not used. On the contrary, I believe that real talent doesn't go away when not in use; it just goes dormant until it's reawakened. Sometimes it can even get better after a time away. **Trust that if you've got it, you've got it. But remember that what you actually do with it is up to you.**

There are many other factors that influence what you eventually attain, including:
- luck
- determination

- single-mindedness
- great people skills
- a talent to network and self-promote
- the skill and self-awareness to reinvent yourself when needed
- good judgment
- a healthy ego, part of sound emotional health
- sound physical health
- a thick skin
- a loving support system.

Any one of these can tip the scales at any time. Talent is simply the price of admission. All the other factors will ebb and flow if you decide that you are in this for the long run, not just a sprint. The art of building a career is learning to control what you can control and letting go of the rest. And yes, having a selective and short memory helps.

STAND BY YOUR INSTINCT

I have often defined talent as having, at its most basic level, very strong and true first instincts. Sometimes our first read of something is the freshest and the most dynamic, and we often spend the rest of our preparation time trying to find our way back to the unsullied quality of that first read.

Case in point: One morning I was stepping out of the shower at 10:00 A.M. when my phone rang. It was my agent asking if I could be at an audition for a film at 11:00 in Century City. Considering that I was soaking wet and Century City was a long drive with thorny parking, I optimistically said it would be tight.

What was the role? The project? My agent knew it was a movie but knew nothing more. "Just get there early and look at the material before you go in."

Get there early? *Fat chance.*

But I dressed, drove, and defeated the parking-matrix beast like a pro. I arrived at 10:55, with five luxurious minutes to look at script pages (called "sides" in the business) for a three-page scene.

The first page was essentially a monologue by my character, who was — drumroll, please — Israeli. Fortunately, my kids had a few Israeli nannies when they were babies, and I'm fairly facile with accents. I felt I had a fighting chance. Four minutes and counting.

I had just finished reading the scene all the way through when the casting assistant appeared. "Are you ready, Michael?"

I put panic aside and smiled. "Absolutely."

I walked into a room and recognized, among the various casting personnel, Robert Duvall. *That would have been good to know going in.* Just the sort of detail that gets dropped in the rush of a morning when some other actor fell out of the audition queue and I got added.

I took my seat. The scene began. I got through it. The accent actually seemed pretty good to me.

The room was silent. William Graham, the director, looked at me and said, "That was perfect."

"Perfect?" I said. "That's not a word I usually hear in rooms like this!"

They laughed, we shook hands all around, and I exited.

Perfect. How did that happen? I had no time to think about it. No time to be nervous. No time to imagine coming face to face with Robert Duvall. I simply had to get there and get it done.

A week later I got a callback — and I panicked. Now I had plenty of time to think, analyze, and overanalyze. I imagined Robert Duvall intently looking at me, seeing my flaws, and judging me. All of the classic actor's insecurities shot up like a geyser.

I thought about it, then called my agent. "No. I'm not going in for the callback."

Before he could talk me out of my choice, I explained: "Look, they said I was perfect, and everyone who's a decision-maker on this film was in the room. I know myself. I know I'll go back there and be *less* than perfect. I could blow it. Make something up. Tell them I'm working. I'm available for the job but not for the callback."

He reluctantly agreed. It was a gutsy move and not one you could likely get away with today. But I claimed the high ground and crossed my fingers.

We went back and forth for a day, my agent telling them that I was filming and couldn't get free (yes, agents do lie, and sometimes even on your behalf).

A week went by in silence. Then the call came. I got the job.

Not only was it a film with Robert Duvall as star and producer, it was also shot in Buenos Aires. I met and worked with remarkable people and spent seven weeks in spectacular Argentina — all because I trusted my first instincts.

Refusing to take the callback could have easily turned out the other way. I could as easily be telling a tale of regret and foolishness here, but that gamble is one that happens again and again in this business.

There was something about the read I gave in that room on that day, when there was no time to think or worry, that really resonated. It was fresh. I felt it was good. They felt it, too. And when the director said, "Perfect," I felt that, too. I knew I was on to something. When it's right, it's right. Know it, and protect that knowledge.

The ironic twist? After all that, my character's big scene was cut from the movie. That's show business! In spite of that, *The Man Who Captured Eichmann* remains one of the best film experiences I ever had.

THE VIRUS OF SELF-DOUBT

Nothing has more confidence than no talent. Yes, sometimes ignorance is bliss. The rest of us battle with issues of confidence and self-doubt every day. It can be a little skirmish or an all-out war. It's a very common part of being a creative artist.

Self-doubt can, however, become a recurring virus... a small, infectious agent that lives in you and pops up every now and then, reactivating just when you thought it was gone for good, just to remind you that it's there. The delicate state of the actor's confidence is always vulnerable to the virus of self-doubt, which tends to flare up at the most inconvenient times: auditions, opening nights, network testing, "chemistry" reads, and agent meetings.

Consider yourself blessed (and very lucky) if you are among those rare people who simply possess enormous confidence at every turn — no matter which way the wind is blowing. I think this form of self-possession is probably there from the womb. But if you're not one of those people, know that even the most successful artists are plagued by fear of failure, self-doubt, and periods of darkness. In fact, many times the greater the talent, the greater the self-doubt.

Artists are often highly self-reflective, a process that can open the door to the sort of deep exploration that may be painful, vulnerable, and truthful — a perfect breeding ground for self-doubt. And the virus knows no bounds. Many of the most successful people I know are plagued by this from time to time.

Recognizing that these thoughts simply go with the territory is the first step toward identifying them for what they are. Then you can work through them — instead of letting them work you.

"The worst thing for an actor is self-judgment. Try to find that thing in you that knows you're a good actor. Find a way to hang on to that. I know that if I can hold my head up and say I like my work, I'm okay. If I can't, and I'm worried about 'them,' then I'm screwed."

— GARY ROSS, writer / producer / director

BE TRUE TO YOURSELF

When I was cast in *The Man Who Captured Eichmann*, starring and produced by Robert Duvall, he arranged for a dinner with cast members. He just wanted to sit with us and get to know us a bit before we traveled to Buenos Aires to shoot — a thrill for everyone. The conversation was far-ranging, friendly, and eventually turned to politics. Dangerous territory!

I had heard that Duvall was a pretty conservative guy, so when he laughingly said to me, "You're not one of those Hollywood liberals, are you?" I wasn't sure exactly how to answer. Was he trying to figure out if I was like him? Or did he already suspect that I wasn't and was trying to see if I would be true to myself?

I mustered my courage and said, "Yes, Bob, I'm afraid I am." He looked at me for a little too long (with that steely Duvall stare), then finally broke into a big grin. "Well, that's just fine." And it was.

The storm passed with my integrity and his professionalism both intact.

REFRAME DIMINISHING WORDS

I know actors who suffer from too much humility. "What are you up to?" I ask.

"I'm in a little play."

A little play? Try: "I'm in this terrific new play. You should come and see it. Do you want me to try to get you a ticket?"

I say to another actor, "Tell me about this film you're in."

"Oh, that? Ultra-low-budget. Probably straight to video."

Or maybe the start of something new. How about: "It was real guerrilla-style filmmaking by a great group of people. I had a blast and met an actor who's also creating original material. We're collaborating on a new script"?

How you frame your experiences — to yourself as well as other people — matters. Those innocent replies send a message. **In a business and craft that depends so much on confidence, those small words can add up to self-fulfilling prophecies.**

Instead of diminishing your efforts, give yourself the respect you deserve. Focus on what you're learning, the experiences you're gaining, the people you're meeting. The process of pursuing your art and craft matters. Acknowledge to yourself that what you're trying to do is difficult. And remember that you have just as much of a shot at success as anyone — as long as *you* believe it.

THE POWER OF A COMPLIMENT

I will never forget the kindness of James Bridges — a wonderful writer / director of noteworthy films including *The China Syndrome*, *The Paper Chase*, and *Urban Cowboy*. He directed me in one of my first feature films, *Perfect*, which starred the young John Travolta and Jamie Lee Curtis.

I shot a week on *Perfect*, and it was months later that I was called into the studio to loop some of my lines. James was out of town, but he called the studio to speak to me. He apologized for not being there with me, though I knew that directors are rarely present for this process. He sincerely thanked me for my work in the film and told me how good I was in the final cut.

Aside from the fact that we actors love a compliment, I was impressed that he took the time to know when I was going to be in the studio, let alone call and talk to me. I'm not certain he did this for every actor, but I imagine he did for most. This personal touch was one of his very best qualities and made me feel appreciated and important for that brief time. He died shortly after that, relatively young, but I remember his kindness to this day.

The personal touch. It's absolutely required. If our handmade art is not personal, then what is it?

EXPLORATION

NAME YOUR FEARS

In the first part of this book, you explored how you define success. Just as importantly, you need to get clear about what you fear.

No magic here. Just write down the things that stop you in your tracks. What cranks up your anxiety and fires up your self-doubt? They can be small or large. As you work on this, don't ignore or overlook what comes to mind, even if it seems strange or even silly.

Fears beg for recognition, one way or another. Looking your fears in the eye is the first step in shifting the power they have in your creative life.

CULTIVATE A TRUTH-TELLER

If you have talent and you love this pursuit, then you owe it to yourself to develop it. You don't want to live your life with a lot of "what ifs."

What if I had really tried?

What if I had committed to tough it out in L.A.? Or New York?

What if I hadn't fallen back on that backup plan?

What if I hadn't listened to all those who discouraged me?

What if...?

Talent is a gift. Not everyone has this gift. But sometimes you need someone to remind you of this. Someone to give you the perspective you can't get by yourself.

Get that by cultivating a truth-teller in your life, someone with compassion who will level with you. Someone who knows you. Someone to remind you of your talent. Someone to give you the particular kick in the ass you need to push through to the next level of self-knowledge that is the core of an artistic life and career.

GET SPECIFIC WITH GOALS

I find that many beginning actors have ambitions and goals that may seem clear, but in fact aren't very specific. Do any of these sound familiar?

I just want to be represented.

I want to book my first costarring role.

I just want to be seen.

I need to get great feedback or my manager will dump me.

I have to get some decent pictures.

But in the chaotic business of entertainment, you'll never achieve specific success without a specific goal. General goals lead to general results. They are unfocused, fuzzy, and conveniently easy to back away from.

A case in point: When I arrived in L.A. in 1983, *Hill Street Blues* was the show everyone wanted to be on. It was smart and innovative in format, with superb writing, directing, and acting. At that time, it was television's high watermark.

This show truly changed television, and I said to myself: *I want to be a part of that.* My goal was very specific: I wanted to be on *Hill Street Blues.* This was the show that every other good actor wanted to be on — many of them with more years in L.A. than I had, with stronger résumés, perhaps better agents, and deeper contacts. But I hadn't uprooted myself and moved West to shoot for the middle.

We are taught that the art of acting is supposed to be about the process, not the result. Like it or not, the business of acting is all about the result, and this time I went straight for it. I focused it firmly on my horizon and worked backwards. I found out who cast the show and learned who some of the directors were. I knew one of the writers (a great surprise to me), quickly found an agent, and tried to figure out who else I knew who could further connect me to this great enterprise. For me, this wasn't about being on a trendy show. This was about being on a *great* show — and being seen in that light. It was about being on a show that smart people in our business watched, a program liked by the real decision-makers.

I worked it and eventually got several auditions for the show — and didn't book one. "That's normal," I was told. It didn't feel normal to me. It felt like failure. "They don't keep bringing you back unless they like you," I was told. More conventional wisdom, but winning the silver or bronze medal just didn't cut it for me. On my fourth or fifth audition, I finally booked the role and went on to play many more roles on Steven Bochco's cutting-edge shows.

Having a very specific goal focused me and gave a forward motion to my efforts. Just hoping to book your first costar or guest-star role is not enough. Instead, imagine yourself where you want to be — on a specific show or with a specific show-runner or director. Imagine yourself — your talent — in a *specific* world that suits you. See the endpoint and then work backwards.

Will you always achieve it? Perhaps. Perhaps not now. Perhaps not ever. This is reality. No one said this would be easy. **General goals lead to a lot of "almosts." But focusing your efforts in a very specific way will lead you to something.** You will meet fellow travelers. You will forge alliances, both personal and professional.

THE FACE OF SUCCESS

In our business, there are no cookie-cutter templates for success. Some people are simply discovered. The vast majority have to work harder at it, using every resource available to us as artists and self-promoters. Unlike other industries, there is no clear-cut career ladder to climb.

Still, we have to be able to imagine success. I've observed that actors who have a successful parent, sibling, or friend of the family have a clearer idea of their own success. They've seen what success looks and feels like, up close and personal. They've seen it happen, so they know that it's achievable. By osmosis, they've had a chance to understand the realities of becoming successful, a sort of mental preparation that gives them a better shot at it.

Look around for role models for your own success. It might be someone you know personally or someone you admire in the business. Learn what motivates them, how they stay focused, what they do in the face of failure, how they view where they are in their own life path. You may discover that the face of success looks very different than you imagined. It may even look more like your own.

SHOOT FOR THE MOON

I once taught an acting seminar at the Hawaii International Film Festival with the extraordinary actress Mary McDonnell. At the end of the workshop, an older gentleman who had been auditing all week and paying very close attention approached me with some thoughtful questions. We talked, and finally I asked him, "Do I know you? You seem so familiar."

"Well, I was an actor for many years. You might recognize my face." And indeed I did. "I never really did much," he said. "I was so in love with the business that I thought to myself — gee, if I could just make a living at this... and that's all I ever did. Just barely made a living."

Only in his retirement did he gain perspective about the self-limitations of humble ambitions. That story was a real watershed for me. He was so in love with just being in "the game" that he never set his sights high enough. He really didn't want to get to the moon. He was happy just being in outer space.

Shoot for the moon. Understand exactly where you are going. And work at becoming an artist along the way so that when you achieve something great, it feels completely logical.

The bottom line? It's just as easy to shoot for the top as it is to shoot for the middle, and you never know how close you are.

LEARN WHAT YOU CAN, WHEREVER YOU ARE

A confession: Coming from theater to a career in TV and film, I was honestly stunned at how bad my first on-camera work was. I didn't have enough respect for the art of acting onscreen. I shared a snobbery common among stage actors who had never tried acting on camera. Everything I did looked pushed and fake, but I was proud and not willing to settle for mediocrity. I was hungry to learn what I was missing.

Shortly after I moved to L.A., I booked a recurring role on the series *Crazy Like a Fox*, starring Jack Warden. Jack was in his sixties and a revered star. He had been twice nominated for an Oscar, and had starred in landmark films including *From Here to Eternity*, *12 Angry Men*, *Shampoo*, *...And Justice for All*, and *The Verdict*.

Jack was a consummate actor who never played a false note — ever. He was also simply a great guy. I was thrilled to be in his orbit, even for a brief time. Whenever I could, I sat with him to talk and ask questions. He was very generous with his time, his advice, and himself.

Jack was a big sports fan, and we often talked baseball. One day we were talking scores and teams, sitting in our chairs at the periphery of the set. (His chair was embroidered with his name. Mine said GUEST.) The crew was shooting coverage on one of Jack's scenes, but he wasn't in the shot. So instead, we shot the breeze.

Suddenly the director appeared. "Jack, I was wrong. You're going to be in this shot."

Jack got up, calmly took his place, and the scene unfolded. What I saw next was something I never forgot: a master class in film acting. On the set with cameras rolling, Jack was absolutely the same guy as he was when he'd discussed baseball with me. No difference. At all. He seamlessly went from life to performance and back again.

It's not that he wasn't acting when the cameras were rolling. He was. He did all the things that good actors do: listened, responded, thought, took his moments, and had a strategy for his character in the scene. But he had simply let go of the idea of having to be someone else. He had such clarity about himself that it totally rang true on film and in life. **He embodied a full integration of life and art, self-knowledge with ease and confidence.** At that moment I understood an essence of exceptional film acting.

It's not that Jack was incapable of portraying a character unlike himself; he absolutely was. He had the skill and the chops to do most anything, and had done that formative work as a younger actor. But in this moment that I witnessed, he knew how to "be" and knew enough not to "do." Not every actor can find this blending of life and art. But the great ones do, and Jack was one of them.

I was a young actor trying to make the pivot from stage (where you often "do") to the screen (where it is important to "be"). I could have been in the best acting class in the world for years and not have learned that lesson as memorably as I did that day on the set with Jack Warden.

Through the years, I used every film and TV job as an opportunity to learn. I was privileged to work with some very accomplished actors, and I made it a point to watch them — how they played a close-up, how they effortlessly channeled their true selves into each moment, how they creatively managed their downtime between takes, how they stayed alive and imaginative at the end of a 14-hour workday. I gladly attended the "school" of Jack Warden, Robert Duvall, Johnny Depp, James Caan, David Strathairn, Jeffrey Tambor, Brian Cox, Stanley Tucci, and many others.

Everyone you meet has something to teach if you're open to learning. Just as a child learns by watching, so can we. School yourself by watching the actors you aspire to meet — or exceed — in levels of performance, professionalism, and personal indelibility.

FIND THE RIGHT PLACE FOR *YOU*

New York? L.A.? Chicago? Or another continent entirely? For an actor, where you locate yourself can define your career and your life. There's no right answer. There's only the right answer *for you*, and everyone else's opinion be damned.

On a trip to New York, I went to see the Louis Armstrong house, which is now a museum. It's in a humble part of Queens that he was proud to call home. And after my visit I understood why he could give such depth to "What a Wonderful World," a song that is, on the surface, somewhat sappy. When he sang it, he was thinking and singing about this neighborhood he loved so much. He said so himself. The sense of place that Louis Armstrong felt in his home elevated that song from sentimental to profound.

I'm a "full-sun flower" who has thrived in the space (and traffic) of L.A. What others find to be laid back about Los Angeles, I find dynamic, provocative, and inspiring. I love being in New York for a few days, soaking up inspiration, but the New York that assaults the senses exhausts me. Other actors, however, feel just the opposite. New York feeds them all the creative juice they need while L.A. drains their soul.

Find the home base that fits your personality, where you feel supported by the environment and community. It could be right under your nose, or totally across the country, or around the world. Place matters. Change your place, change your destiny.

"It's important as a human being and as an actor to recognize signposts. It's good to have a master plan, but it's like acting — prepare, then let it go. When a signpost appears, it might have your name on it, so look at it."

— Jim Piddock, actor / writer / producer

EVERYTHING YOU'VE HEARD
ABOUT L.A. IS TRUE

I was home on a rare rainy Los Angeles night watching the ultimate film about L.A. and the film business, *Sunset Boulevard*. I recognized many of the old locations, some still unchanged: views of the Chateau Alto Nido Apartments, the Paramount gate, the intersection of Ivar and Franklin in Hollywood. Much of it (amazingly) looks the same.

But of course a great deal has changed. Schwab's is gone, as is Perino's Restaurant — one of L.A.'s premier Golden Era eateries — glimpsed through the window of the fancy Wilshire Boulevard men's store where Norma Desmond buys Joe Gillis an expensive new set of clothes. Then, as today, the seductive qualities of this town, this industry, this way of life still draw hopefuls from all over the world. The many clichés surrounding the emptiness of Hollywood success abound, and the dark, cynical worldview of Joe Gillis is no place to dwell. Yet I find myself unable to stop watching *Sunset Boulevard* no matter how many times I've seen it.

The yearning and the promise of being able to tell stories for a living burns as brightly today as it did when *Sunset Boulevard* was made. I see it in my students. I see it in myself. I've been around this industry and city long enough to recognize the glamour, disappointment, and compromise that inhabit the towering performances of William Holden, Gloria Swanson, and Erich von Stroheim. Despite all the hurdles and flat-out brick walls, I still have to say that I love it all. I love the town, the action, and the wonderful people I have met (and continue to meet).

Everything you've ever heard about Los Angeles is true — all of it. But there are also about 10,000 other things about it that are also true that are surprising, strange, contradictory, exciting, and downright inspiring. Venture out. Meet it. It doesn't slap you across the face every day and say "wake up!" the way New York does. It entices you with sunshine, relentlessly blue skies, and the ongoing seduction of new possibilities.

UNDER-PROMISE AND OVER-DELIVER

One of the most important lessons I learned early in life, probably from my father, was to under-promise and over-deliver. In other words, exceed expectations. Become indispensable by always delivering what you say you will. It's always smart to be a wonderful surprise instead of a disappointment. It's just good business.

When this behavior becomes habit, it also helps in building trust, love, loyalty, and friendship. It's a trait that positively reinforces whatever you say you'll do. Think of it as a craft — a craft for living one's life.

IS IT YOUR TIME?

"Sometimes it's your time. And sometimes it's not your time." My students have heard me say this, and I absolutely believe it. There is an ebb and flow to the creative life that has its own pulse, sometimes exclusive of your best efforts. And this force also exerts influences on *all* aspects of your life. As much forward thrust as we bring to the task, this underlying pattern is as immutable as the ocean tides. We have to make this aspect of life our friend — something we can dance with and something we know will come around when we least expect it with love, encouragement, and maybe a few dollars.

How do we remain enthusiastic and engaged in the face of the low ebbs? The fact is that discouragement and temporary failure are both part of this larger pattern. If you maintain an honest, disciplined, and dedicated effort independent of how the winds are blowing, you will be ready when the fair winds arrive. And they will. You have to trust me on that. I'm old enough to know how this goes.

The creative life is difficult, rewarding, heartbreaking, and exhilarating. And for most of us, there is no choice in this. That's part of what it means to be an Authentic Actor.

If it's what you *must* do, then please do it with a sense of purpose (and a sense of humor — which is also very important). Anything worthy of your talent and efforts takes time, dedication, and sacrifice. I don't believe there are any plausible shortcuts. You've simply got to put in the time.

I've heard young actors opine that it used to be so much easier in my day, as if I was artistically roaming the earth in the Paleolithic era! I have to nicely set them straight. It was *never* easy.

Were the "good old days" better? To be completely honest, they usually do seem better to those of us who are old enough to look back. When I was a young performer, the older veteran actors always groused about how it had been better back in the old days. The fact is that the good old days simply represent our youth — when our lives were less complicated, when passions for everything ran deep, and when we had an unerring sense of mission about what we did. We didn't worry about how long the warranty on our car was — if we even had one.

If you are a young artist, today is the beginning of your good old days. So the question remains: Is *now* your time? I absolutely think it is. You have to understand that there is rarely a visible, direct cause-and-effect nature to what we do. This intangibility is one aspect of its unique magic.

But know this: When things are bad, they will get better. And when things are good, know that they will get worse. They will ebb and flow. And if your sense of purpose remains strong, if your efforts remain dedicated, those ebbs and flows will become *your* "good old days."

Hector Elizondo (*Chicago Hope, Grey's Anatomy, Pretty Woman*) is one of the wisest, most generous actors in our business. The perspective he shared with my class was a manual on how to live as an artist, understand your value as a commodity, and retain your humanity throughout. Hector is a bright light, and his friendship is something I treasure.

Jeffrey Tambor (*Transparent, Arrested Development, The Hangover*) is a dear friend and a consummate artist. He embodies so much of what being an Authentic Actor is about: highly developed skill mated with an absolutely clear sense of self and worldview. Jeff has taught me a lot and always challenged me to be better, for which I am eternally grateful. On the night he visited class, we laughed for most of the two hours!

Michael Langham (1919–2011) was one of the most acclaimed directors in the English-speaking theater world. As Artistic Director of the Guthrie Theater, he offered me a contract after taking notice of me in a production of *The Three Sisters* directed by Charles Nolte. Michael's endorsement meant more to me than he ever knew. I was very lucky to have been in his world for a brief time. An extraordinary man and inspired artist, he set a standard that anyone who was a part of his incandescent productions never forgot.

Writer/director John Sayles (here on location in Bohol, Philippines) has a talent for creating a "tribe" on every set, which brings out the best in everyone.

Limbo (1999) was my third film with iconic writer-director John Sayles. John makes it easy for actors, because the writing is always extraordinary. He also writes a detailed biography of each character in his films, no matter the size of the part. That backstory enriches every actor's work — one reason his films are filled with memorable performances. A true auteur.

John Sayles' *Eight Men Out* (1988) is considered one of the all-time great baseball films and my first of four movies with John. Here I am as attorney Albert Austrian schooling the ballplayers on their legal strategy (James Read and John Cusack in the shot, with David Strathairn, Charlie Sheen, and others around the table).

Bounce (2000) starred Ben Affleck and Joe Morton — both extraordinarily generous actors on and off the set.

Medium (2007) was standard network-TV fare with little time to shoot and no time to rehearse. Because of this, my core qualities as an actor came to the forefront in this cauldron. All the more reason to be as authentic as possible.

Playing opposite Jeff Goldblum in *Mini's First Time* (2006) was always fun and frequently scary, because I never knew where we were going! To say he kept it fresh is an understatement. But I rarely had so much fun or felt as loose on a set. Jeff is a great collaborator and co-conspirator!

Playing scenes with Alec Baldwin in *Mini's First Time* (2006) was intense and emotionally full. Alec is a great actor, a thoroughbred. You have to play at his level, or you'll disappear. I was able to do that, and it felt right.

Poodle Springs (1998) had an amazing pedigree: script by Tom Stoppard (based on Raymond Chandler's last, unfinished novel featuring the Philip Marlowe character), directed by Bob Rafelson (*Five Easy Pieces, The Postman Always Rings Twice*) and starring James Caan. He made every scene real, loose, collaborative, and fun.

Acting in *Seinfeld* was probably the most fun I ever had on a set — a total blast. Watching Jerry Seinfeld, Jason Alexander, Julia Louis-Dreyfus, and Michael Richards rehearsing, laughing, and creating on their feet all week, I knew I would remember this for a very long time. Being able to work with them was icing on the cake — a joyful privilege.

Between my first audition and being actually cast in *Winchell* (1998), a year passed. I had actually forgotten about it when the call came in! Directed by Paul Mazursky (*Bob & Carol & Ted & Alice*, among so many others) and starring Stanley Tucci, this was an exercise in patience that paid off handsomely.

Alfred Molina (*Chocolat, Boogie Nights*) is a giant of an actor, and his ever-present humanity is the prism through which all his characters are brought to life. Fred's performance in *Red* (Mark Taper Forum, Los Angeles, 2010) remains one of the greatest I've witnessed on stage. Speaking to my students, he was his usual self — humble, self-effacing, and ferociously intelligent.

Ron Perlman (*Hellboy, Drive*), one of the very best actors of my generation, has been a good friend for many years. He spoke to that night's class with tremendous clarity and passion about acting, life, and professionalism.

The night he visited class, Gary Ross (*The Hunger Games*, *Big*) schooled us in the passion and vision it takes to persevere and succeed. Gary spoke about acting from his perspective as a writer and director, as well as a former student of acting. For someone who has succeeded at the highest commercial levels in the film industry, Gary retains a zeal for the craft, a passion for the art.

21 Jump Street (1987–1991) started as an offbeat series created by Stephen J. Cannell, one of the great forces in television at the time. I played a crooked politician in several episodes and worked alongside a very young Johnny Depp. Even in this still from 1989, his natural charisma is evident. Johnny had a special relationship with the camera that endures to this day. It was fun to be around a new comet in the sky.

Top casting director Debra Zane (*American Beauty*, *The Hunger Games*) tells it like it is. She was the first guest at my studio class and returned five years later to let students in on the reality of auditions, the importance of fearlessness, and avoiding pay-to-be-seen casting workshops.

The Disney feature *Iron Will* (1994) was directed by the talented and tenacious Charlie Haid and starred Kevin Spacey right before he exploded as a star. Kevin was the most ambitious, self-possessed actor I had ever encountered. But, he was also wonderful to work with — funny, loose, collaborative, and always entertaining. When you can have fun in sub-zero temperatures while working with animals, that's a great shoot.

Working with Robert Duvall in *The Man Who Captured Eichmann* (1996) was a career highlight. I had heard he was difficult. He was not. He was, however, the most prepared actor I've ever encountered. He was fully ready with his best work on Take 1 — and might be unhappy if we got to Take 4. If you kept up with him, he was amazingly generous and supportive.

5

THE AUDITION

They'll know it when they see it.

MORE CONTROL AND LESS FEAR

All actors have at least one thing in common: Everyone struggles with auditions. If you designed a minefield for actors, it would look a lot like the TV or film audition — what I call "office acting." Little preparation time or guidance, messy logistics, often meaningless feedback. Rarely do we feel that the audition experience lets us fully show our talent. It can feel more like target shooting in the dark, and you're the one who leaves wounded.

Here's how it looks: You found out about the audition just 24 hours ago. Now you're stuck in traffic on the way to a casting office at a major studio. Breathe deeply. It's no problem! You knew traffic would be horrific, so you left home in plenty of time. You can use that extra drive time to go over the scenes. Acting while driving (hands free, of course) is an L.A. tradition.

You pull up to the studio gate, and for some reason the security guard doesn't have your name. It takes a few calls, but finally you're in. The guard sends you to park at the far end of the lot, about three blocks away from where you need to be. You hadn't planned on this, and now you're wondering if you'll be late.

C'mon... stay focused.

It's 103 degrees outside, and you're wearing your best business clothes. You walk those three blocks in the blazing sun and try to mind-trick yourself into a no-sweat mode. It almost works.

By the time you're inside the building, you know you need to freshen up before walking into The Room. Finding a bathroom is its own adventure. Now you're certain you'll be late.

As soon as you get to the waiting room, you're up! You're announced, and you walk into a room crowded with a casting crew at the end of their day, game but tired. They've already seen dozens of actors. The air conditioning is blasting away, and within a minute you're freezing. Did you just see your own breath?

Turns out they only want to see you do the second scene (of three you diligently prepared). *What?* Your character has a single line in that scene. *That can't be right.* The other scenes are juicier. *What are they thinking?*

You can see they want to wrap up the session. *Have they already cast the role? Is this just a formality? Are offers already out? Focus!*

With one line, there will have to be a lot of reacting. The weary reader gives you absolutely nothing and rushes the scene, which admittedly isn't much to begin with. But you shake it all off, focus on the work, and say your one line:

"Ready, babe?"

The casting director doesn't look up, but asks you do it again with "more." *More?* "You know... give it a little edge." She finally makes eye contact. *What does that look mean?*

So you say it again, with what you think is some version of "more," some extra dose of "edge."

"Ready, babe?"

Nothing. Crickets. You thank the room, and you're out the door — hoping you won't be late to your serving job.

On the way to your car you kick yourself for feeling nervous, not connecting, or not [fill in the blank]. You get back on the road and do it once more. You *nail* it. Yes, you just did your best reading — in the car. Another L.A. tradition.

You can't control much of what happens in an audition. That makes it even more critical that **you control your own attitude and approach to the process**. That gives you the best chance of making an impact within your narrow window of opportunity.

"When you walk into an audition, don't
talk yourself out of the chance."

— MARK PIZNARSKI, director / producer / writer

THE HINT OF MORE

If your talent is like a lyric poem, then think of TV and film auditions as haiku, a type of poetry that creates a vivid experience with very few words. A haiku doesn't say everything, but it says *enough*. It makes the point and hints at even more.

Another way to think of it: If a full performance is a painting, an audition is the pencil sketch. The challenge is how to create a sketch that intrigues people enough to want to see what the full painting would look like. That depends on communicating your point of view, your understanding of the text, and your blink-of-an-eye factor in that very short space of time. **Your clear point of view — your personal indelibility — helps to cut through the sameness.** And if you can bring that into the room with you, you may get the chance to show them the painting.

FIVE ELEMENTS OF KILLING IN AN AUDITION

We know all the obstacles. So how can an actor hope to cut through the noise, make a lasting impression, and possibly book the job? How can an actor stay focused through all the little indignities and inconveniences that can completely undermine self-confidence? Actors who succeed in auditions do several things that you can do, too:

1. **Treat every audition opportunity as a job.** Prepare for it and conduct yourself with that inner narrative of professionalism.
2. **Discover the changes in the scene.** Create your road map for the scene and the character within it.
3. **Find (and earn) a moment.** To communicate your indelible self, find the moment in the material that is unique to you.
4. **Change the rhythm of the audition room.**
5. **Create space for your authentic self to be in that room as an equal.** See yourself as a collaborator in solving the casting director's problem.

   Really? All of that? Every time?

   Ideally, yes. But we're human. We come up short some days. Then anger, disappointment, and the occasional beating-up of self are part of the mad bargain of pursuing an acting career. It's essential, however, to get past that — and get past it quickly. **The actor's "head game" is at least as important as talent.**

   Your solid mental game is what enables you to bring your own indelible self into the transaction — and make no mistake, auditions are transactions. As an actor, I know this from the inside. As a coach and teacher, I see it clearly from the outside.

ROAD MAP OF AN AUDITION SCENE

What, essentially, is an audition? It's an opportunity to communicate a compressed, immediate, and dynamic version of yourself and your character — one that is revealed the minute you walk through the door. "Office acting" is tricky, and it requires a special kind of self-assured, self-aware confidence.

Scenes chosen for TV and film auditions usually show some important change, conflict, or dilemma in a character's arc. These are moments that define the character, and everyone in the room wants to see it in your work in real time. An audition must be smart, intelligent, and excellent — but *compressed.* That doesn't mean fast. It means *emotionally immediate.* Your job is to find that truth in the scene in a way that's personal and unique to you.

You do that by creating a road map of the scene. Every scene (or series of scenes) you get will have a trajectory — a direction it is taking. This can be discovered by paying close attention to where the scene changes and where your character evolves or transitions. This is sometimes rather obvious stuff, but I am always surprised that so many actors seem to ignore it or miss it entirely.

Like water flowing downhill, the trajectory of a scene or scenes will take a certain course naturally. And, given the fact that there is so little preparation time, many actors will make the most obvious choices. The actor's job is to honor what the writers intended while still imbuing the material with as much of their personal DNA as they can. This means finding the less obvious choices — ones that are intelligent and unique to you but still serve the needs of the scene.

What is the scene about? Start with the obvious, then open up your thinking to large concepts or ideas. Is the scene about jealousy? Guilt? Honor? Sex? As an actor in the scene, you cannot actually play these concepts, but this macro-perspective gives you the freedom to see the scene from the outside and see its function within the story. Then in the playing of it, you must discover even just a moment or two to play the scene "on the margins of the page" — not "down the middle," where most everyone else will play it because of lack of time or (more likely) lack of imagination.

Great actors don't make obvious choices. They make personal choices that (if well executed) can become indelibly great choices. They look for and find values that go beyond what the scene appears to be about. Look for those less obvious choices.

Find and earn your moment. In *The Godfather*, Marlon Brando's Don Corleone has a scene in which he explains his idea of friendship to the undertaker Bonasera. As this threatening scene unfolds, he holds and affectionately pets a cat on his lap. Did Brando plan this? No. That animal was a stray that lurked around the Paramount lot, but in Brando's hands, in that specific scene where he is quietly making points about loyalty and revenge — his gentle stroking of the cat creates an unforgettable duality in his character.

Can you bring a cat into the audition room with you? Not literally. But you can always look for that unique opportunity in the scene, something that is fresh, original, unexpected, and personal to you.

THE AUDITION IS YOUR JOB

Let's be honest. We all want it! *We all want the job!* We want that phone call telling us we have an offer. If we didn't want it, we wouldn't be human.

But beware the turn from *wanting* it into *desperately needing* it. There are always plenty of external factors pushing the actor there: You need one more job for your SAG-AFTRA insurance. You sense your manager is losing confidence in you. Your kid needs braces. Tuition (for both kids) is due. You haven't booked in a while and your momentum is stalling. Your significant other is pressuring you to get a "regular job."

When actors bring even a whiff of desperation into the room, the audition's over before it even started. The people in the room can smell it coming all the way from the parking structure. **It's your job to change that "please pick me" narrative and see every audition as a job. Period.**

You have a job — it just happens to be on the Warner Bros. lot at 4:45 on a Thursday afternoon in Building 142, Room 10. And you actually may get a chance to do that job again for money, on a sound-stage, or on location. But for now, it's your job at 4:45 on Thursday. Your job. Go in there and do it.

"Know that the casting director is not the actor's enemy. We invited you in. We want you to succeed. We're hoping you're the answer. We are truly in the process together."

— DEBRA ZANE, casting director

WHO ARE "THEY" AND WHAT DO "THEY" WANT?

Trying to find out what "they" want is a fool's errand. Yes, there's a character breakdown — and within that are several hints about what the casting people are saying they want. Take from that what you can, but I find that it's equally — if not more — important to think about what *you* want.

Here's the reality I learned the hard way about the mythical "they":

1. Whoever "they" are, they often don't truly know what they want.

2. What they think they want is fluid and changeable, sometimes even at the casting session. They are "in the moment" as well.

3. Like ours, their process can be subject to compromise and chaos.

4. And, as clichéd as it sounds, they'll know it when they see it.

A long time ago, I came to the liberating conclusion that what they really want is for you to come into the room and solve their problem. What they'd love to see is someone with a unique actor's fingerprint mated with skill, professionalism, intelligence, and preparation. They want to check this casting problem off their list and move on to the next one.

SHOW THEM WHO YOU ARE

A young actor came to me for help with an important audition. He was overwhelmed with trying to show them everything he knew in a few short minutes. So many emotional colors! So much talent! Such a range — he wanted them to see it all! It was exhausting for him, and strangely ineffective for me watching him. **In his quest to show everything, he was showing virtually nothing.**

We want results. We crave acceptance. If we jump through enough hoops and dance faster than everyone else, we'll get both, right? But the missing element in all this is *you.*

Show them all your tricks; get a gold star in your workbook. Terrific. There are dozens of actors before and after you who will do the same. But none of them can walk in the room and be you. So, if you show nothing of yourself, you've drastically shortchanged the transaction. It's your job to somehow change that room and become the solution to their problem. You do that by inviting them to *your* party.

I finally said to him, "This is all wonderful, but *who the hell are you?*" He was a bit stunned. He would rather hammer away at surface dynamics than reveal something of himself. And without that revelation, it's all just a little dance in line with dozens of other little dances that are, in the end, forgettable. **All the talent in the world rarely overcomes a lack of personal connection.**

Make it personal. Show them who you are. Take that risk. Have fun. This is true of auditions, job interviews, and lunch. If you don't enjoy it, no one else will.

"I cannot think of a more useless thing than an audition class. It doesn't teach you to act. It teaches you how to game the system. And that only increases your fear while weakening your sense of efficacy and agency as an actor."

— GARY ROSS, writer / producer / director

SET YOUR STANDARDS — TAKE THE RISK

Make no mistake: The audition is a transaction in which you are an equal. Your point of view is valid, or you wouldn't be in that room. But your first duty is not to please them. It's easy to get lost in the pursuit of pleasing them, a path to rarely pleasing yourself.

Your first duty is to dynamically bring the character to life in a way that's personal to you and honors the intent of the writers and the world they have created. If you enter the transaction with anything less than that, you devalue your work. Frankly, you might as well have stayed home. Blunt words, but this is the truth of the matter.

It's not easy to create this confident narrative, especially when pressing real-life needs muddy the waters. But you simply must; you have no choice. You're an actor! Pretend!

Pretend you are confident. I'm dead serious. I firmly believe that arbitrary action can take hold and become your new narrative. Actor, friend, and mentor Jeffrey Tambor thinks of his auditions this way: "If you should choose to pay me, this is how I would do it." Strong. Confident. An equal. The solution. A collaborator.

So, let this truth set you free. **Take a big creative shot.** What's the worst thing that could happen? Rejection? No. Humiliation? No. The worst that could happen is that you could be mediocre. Sometimes even being wonderfully wrong is far better and can signify a risk taker, an explorer, maybe even an artist.

Focus on doing a great piece of work to your own standards first. Their standards may be amazingly high or amazingly low. Frankly, it doesn't matter. Your standards have to become high and remain high, inviting them into your world.

One of the very best auditions I ever had was for Joel and Ethan Coen, reading for the role of Stan Grossman in *Fargo*. I did it to my standards completely. They laughed. They were surprised. They were engaged. They said, "That was great. Terrific work. We never thought of him that way. That was really very, very good."

Did I get the role? No. Did I do exactly what I wanted? Yes. Would I have done anything differently? Absolutely not. My job was to illuminate that character in a way that was personal and unique to me. Not a booking but, within the larger story of my life as an actor, a real success story.

So, rather than wondering what "they" are looking for, ask this: What are *you* looking for? Prepare the audition that leaves you thinking, "I'd hire me."

Ultimately your job is to be indelible. Unforgettable. That's it. The surest route to this indelible impact is doing the work in front of you in a way that's immediate and authentic to you. What "they" want is you. They just don't know it yet and will never know it unless the authentic you comes into that transaction.

To be clear, I am not advocating being obstinately tone-deaf to what people in the casting room want (or think they want). Look for clues — absolutely. Get a feel for the world you are entering — yes. But never lose sight of the fact that your personal take on the work, your artistic contribution, is valuable, valid, and needed. It's really all you've got that distinguishes you from the crowd.

Think about how this clear-eyed acknowledgment of your value might be integrated not only into your career but also your life. And justify that empowerment with dedication. If you engage in this process as an artist, what "they" will want might very possibly be you.

FILMING YOUR AUDITION

Although the talent business is still largely based in Los Angeles and New York, film and TV production is everywhere. Tax incentives are taking productions to places like Louisiana, South Carolina, New Mexico, and Vancouver. The global cinema business has thriving industries churning out productions on every continent except Antarctica. Not being in the same room as the casting director is no longer an impediment to getting yourself seen for far-flung roles. Hugh Laurie shot his first audition for *House* in Namibia, from his hotel room.

What's your opportunity? Filming your audition gives you more control over the result. You have the opportunity to get it right, doing a few takes until you feel you've got it where you want it. No longer do you have to feel like you have to nail it in the room on the first take. To some extent you can take more time with this until you are happy with what you've sent off to the producers, wherever they may be. You can leave those "I did my best take in the car on the way home" days behind you.

Here's the challenge: It's true that in this new and growing way of auditioning, you are more in charge of the final product. However, be aware that **this is not an endeavor for the perfectionist in you.** I have seen actors do their best work on take one or two and totally lose the performance by take seven or eight. You lose your freshness and you lose your judgment. Have someone you trust artistically (coach, acting teacher, significant other) be a part of this process.

The preparation is the same as it would be for a live audition. Your work still needs to be examined and ready by the time you are going to shoot — just as it would be were you walking into an audition room on a studio lot. But, as Voltaire and many other philosophers over centuries have advised: **Perfect is the enemy of good.** Remember this when filming your auditions. Perfection can also be the enemy of freshness, a sense of discovery, and nuance in your work.

Technical note: I know a lot of people say that it doesn't really matter how it looks — just shoot it on your phone. To this, I say a resounding *no*. It does matter how good it looks and sounds. Find a way to shoot in the most technically advanced way possible within a budget that makes sense for you. Be creative. Many actors I know have great setups at home, and with today's technology it's within reach for many. Even smartphones are getting good enough to sometimes suffice.

You can also tap into the specialists who film auditions for actors. Some of them are quite good, but don't believe the advertisements. Ask people you trust for recommendations.

Keep your performance fresh, and let it shine through the quality of picture and sound. You want your work to be seen in the best light possible — literally! Technology is an ally in getting yourself seen, and used wisely it's one fewer reason for a casting director to say "no."

FACE TO FACE

I once had to meet director Stephen Frears for a role in his film, *The Grifters*. I was told to prepare nothing. "Mr. Frears just wants to meet you." I guessed that he assumed that if you'd made it this far you were a good actor, but he still needed to meet you. He wanted to feel your presence in the room — human to human.

When I was escorted into his office, he was lying on a couch after lunch, crumbs dotting his sweater. He was a rumpled presence, like an unmade bed. He just chatted with me while he sipped some tea. We spoke for at least 20 minutes — a good and substantive conversation about everything *but* the film! He just wanted to see me, have a sense of me in the room, and feel out who I was. On that basis alone, I was cast in *The Grifters*. This is a sign of a very confident and intuitive director.

What is it about meeting face to face that so powerfully attracts (or repels)? It's beyond words.

THE UPS AND DOWNS OF FEEDBACK

What did the casting director think? Getting feedback is an obsession among many agents, managers, and actors. But feedback is a mixed bag that can be both useful and meaningless. A lot is lost in translation from the scribbled notes of a casting director to their assistant to your agent or manager to you.

Take it all with a large grain of salt. The most valuable part? **Look and listen for patterns.** "She's way too serious about herself." "He really doesn't listen." If you get a consistent note like this, then it's time to pay attention, consider, and correct. Bad patterns need to be addressed. But don't be afraid to leave the rest behind, especially if it's distracting you from what's next.

Move on. Focus your attention on the road forward.

LET IT GO!

What do you do after an audition? Let it go. Try to forget it ever happened and move on to the next. Fretting over it and obsessing about it accomplishes absolutely nothing. In fact, it feeds your already simmering anxiety. **Let it go.**

You do your best, and either you get the job or you don't. It often has nothing to do with you, or how you might have auditioned. We can't know all the forces at play.

I auditioned for the HBO film *Winchell*, a biopic of legendary gossip columnist and reporter Walter Winchell. I went in and read for the film's director, the acclaimed Paul Mazursky. The meeting went extraordinarily well. He was digging my take on this part. We laughed and seemed to have an immediate shorthand with each other.

Paul gave me several adjustments and worked with me in great detail. I left there thinking, "I've got this; I nailed it."

My agent followed up, but we heard nothing. And followed up again and heard nothing. One last time, six weeks later: again, nothing.

Sometimes Hollywood's way of saying "no" is simply saying nothing. I started second-guessing my memory of the audition. *I must have misread the situation.*

The only thing I could do was forget about it and move on. I did, and nearly a year later I got the call. I'd booked the part.

Huh? Where were they for the last 12 months? They couldn't have called?

I found out that elements had fallen through that delayed the production. The script was being rewritten, and they had a new star to play Winchell, Stanley Tucci. These weren't things they needed to discuss with me. While I experienced silence, they were managing their own version of the chaos it takes to get any film or TV show made.

So to those who obsess about feedback or results, I say again: Let it go. It's out of our hands, and there are unknown forces at play that swirl around projects and affect their destiny.

I wasn't wrong about my first meeting with Mazursky. We did connect, but I had no idea what else he was dealing with. We can only control what we can control: our work, our attitude, our dedication, our professionalism. And once in a while, what you let go comes back to you.

6

THE ART OF CAREER

Know when to say fuck 'em.

KNOW WHAT YOU'RE WORTH

Is everything we do in life a transaction? I don't have an easy answer for that, but I tend to think it may be. Even if you are acting out of the goodness of your heart, I happen to believe that it may come back to you in unexpected ways. So, even though we sometimes do things expecting nothing in return, a transaction takes place at some point in the future. Call it karma, or whatever makes sense for you.

It often comes down to putting a number on the table. What are you worth? That's a separate question from what someone will pay. It's also a separate question from how badly you need what they might give you. Add to that the fact that the entertainment marketplace itself is in upheaval. New media, small indie projects, nonunion work, union work... as everyone becomes more entrepreneurial, the notion of "value" becomes a moving target.

Know this: **Everybody has a number. Some people are just never given the opportunity to find out what it is.**

A long time ago I had an old friend who used to sell me antique watches. Harry was a third-generation jeweler and watchmaker, and taught me everything about buying and selling. He taught me what things are worth. I'd say, "Harry, how much do you want for these?"

He'd say, with a sly laugh, "As much as I can get, kid." And there were times when I'd make him an offer on something, and he'd stop me — teaching me at the same time — and say, "That's too much, kid; you'll never get your money out."

But as artists we are not really selling *things*. We are placing value on little pieces of ourselves. Can you put an accurate price tag on 30 years of experience? What's the monetary value of all the hard work, sacrifice, and long hours? *What's your dream worth?*

Every once in a while, an actor will get a job that unexpectedly pays wonderfully. You're on a movie, all your scenes are to be shot outside, and it rains for weeks... and weeks. You just keep getting paid. Your dedication over the entire course of the actor's journey has earned you this money, too.

I came face to face with this when I was up for a major studio film. The offer was very low. Fortunately, my manager Bruce Tufeld was very passionate about respecting what I was really worth. He gave me the courage to value myself more highly. Our answer to the deal wasn't "no," but it also wasn't "yes." In the end, Bruce was able to negotiate a figure quite a bit higher than the studio's original offer — something closer to the number I had in mind.

Remember that those studio dealmakers aren't placing a value on your *artistic* self. A low offer isn't a sign of what they think of your talent. They're just trying to get every piece of their project in place for as little money as possible. If you're willing to accept a low offer, why should they pay you more?

Most artists would do what we do for free because we love it. That gives us a tendency to sell ourselves short. Make sure you have a manager, agent, or other advisor to remind you what you're worth in the marketplace and help you negotiate to get it. Those dollars and cents on the contract and in your bank account are not a measure of your artistic merit, but they do help support your pursuit of a place in the industry. You bring unique value that no one else can. Don't forget it.

PILOT SEASON: THE BEST AND THE WORST OF TIMES

Pilot season is a time of big opportunity and even bigger disappointment. For those fortunate enough to be a part of this barely controlled madness, consider this: The very best hitters in baseball have a 70% failure rate at the plate. However, they fully believe that they can hit the ball every time — and this is the key to their 30% success rate.

Pilot season is an extreme example of how the marketplace in our industry functions. Or doesn't function. Of the hundreds of pilots made every year, very few get on the air, and fewer still have the sticking power to become hits. The failure rate of this clearly insane process probably would not be tolerated in any other business. It's emblematic of the boom-and-bust nature of the entertainment business, a truth since its beginning.

But the process of developing new television shows is in continual flux as new content-creation models emerge, and companies like Hulu and Netflix make shows the way NBC and CBS do. Pilot season will evolve as the television industry adapts to new realities.

How we deal with the inevitable high rate of misses in our business and artistic lives informs how we relate to success. Success is not just the absence of failure. Success is attaining a continuous state of confidence based on belief in our talent, immersion in our work, and deep knowledge of who we are. No one ever said being an artist was easy, especially in the business context of the entertainment industry. But nothing worth doing with passion requires any less. The richness of your artistic life is completely in your hands.

MAKING SENSE OF SUCCESS

Congratulations! You got the job! That's a tremendous feeling. Enjoy it! You've earned the right. One of the greatest moments about a job is getting the phone call that you've booked it. In fact, I've done a few jobs where the high point of the whole experience was getting this call. The actual job might have been less than I'd hoped, but it was a kick to get that call.

Some actors like to keep score. These actors measure their success against others and either feel like a failure or smug in their good fortune. Listen to me clearly: Do not keep score. Every job you get is a small miracle, accomplished against very tough odds. Jobs are hard-earned and can go away in a flash. **Be empathetic toward actors who have not gotten a break, and be happy for those who have.** When a friend of mine books a big job, I take it as a hopeful reminder that the same is possible for me.

Even as you move through your professional career, remember why you wanted a career in the first place. Remember the authentic heart of the amateur — you are acting because you love it. Your challenge in the face of success is to mate the zeal of the amateur with true professionalism.

DEALING WITH REJECTION

You prepared for weeks. You paid for coaching sessions to make sure you had the role down cold. You absolutely killed the audition. Then you get the call that the role went to someone else. "It's not going forward," your manager says.

What happened? What didn't you do? You search the possibilities and land on the idea that the casting director killed your chances. She has her favorites, and you are clearly not among them!

That night you go to a party to get your mind off it, and who shows up? *The casting director*. This is your chance to make sure she knows what a mistake she made.

Hold on... take a break. Count to ten and don't be stupid.

As actors, we deal in the business of dreams, and the road from dream to disappointment can be rather short and abrupt. How do you handle disappointment? What do you do when the wave breaks against you? Does it take a day, a week, or a year to get over it? How gracious can you be to the people who seem to hold so much power over your career?

Some people in the entertainment business (and in life) wear their disappointment and defeat like a yoke around their neck. "I could have been a contender... I could have been somebody." Disappointment and defeat can become a place of comfort, always seeking new friends. Misery loves company, and it can be contagious. My advice: **Be compassionate to those working through a defeat — including yourself — but don't allow yourself to get stuck there.**

And when you run into that casting director, smile and be gracious. Every meeting is a chance to make the impression that will get you a call, whether tomorrow, next month, or next year. It's show business. But it's also human business.

LEARNING TO BE SELECTIVE

The late, great Mary Ellen White was my first agent in Los Angeles, and she taught me the strategy of being selective. At times, she advised me to turn down a role if it wasn't where we agreed I wanted to be or be seen. I trusted her through my bouts of panic.

Turning down work — being selective — on the face of it sure looked like a terrible strategy. In fact it was the opposite. Her thinking was: "They like you, so we're going to wait for something better to come along in that series." She was absolutely correct, even though it felt counterintuitive, especially given our uncertain business.

Will that better role come along tomorrow? She taught me to trust that it would. And when it did, the result was even more empowering.

I believe every actor should always aim for the top and aspire to the best-quality work possible. You absolutely want to be in that top 5% of the great films and TV shows. That's what you signed up for! Becoming selective is part of being a professional, and is essential to valuing your efforts. That starts with being clear about your own criteria for saying yes or no to a role. Shaping your career depends on gaining that clarity and knowledge — and then having the confidence to act on it.

7 REASONS TO TAKE A JOB

The best roles are the ones that give us a chance to do quality work and make a decent living at it. Early in my career, I defined the three top reasons to take a job. They still hold true today.

1. It's a wonderful part — your talents will be showcased in a great light.
2. The money is good — your quote was met or exceeded.
3. The project is so cool that you simply want to be a part of it.

Even today, if a job doesn't fulfill at least one of these requirements, I have to think long and hard before taking it. But there are other reasons that are more about business strategy and real life that can come into play.

4. You want to build or sustain career momentum.
5. You want to become known to key people — such as a producer, director, or casting director — a role being your foot in the door for future projects.
6. You need to pay the bills — a particular pressure if you've got a growing family.
7. You need one more job to keep your SAG-AFTRA eligibility and that health insurance!

Perfect example: I did an Adam Sandler movie! Not one of his good ones, either. I played his father in *Just Go With It*. I was told it was one day's work. My manager said that I should take it, because it's never one day's work on an Adam Sandler movie. They improvise, they expand roles, they create on the spot. He was right; one day turned into twelve days.

I also met and worked with Adam (he was absolutely great), got to dance with Jennifer Aniston (a nice side benefit), and made a good deal of money. Not a bad outcome. Except for one fleeting shot, I was ultimately cut out of the film. But I still get those residuals, and I had the pleasure of working with some rather amazing people. And when there's a mortgage, car payment, school tuition, or credit-card bills coming due, money in the bank is an honorable thing.

SLUMMING WITH A SMILE

Early on in my career, I was a guest star on the original *Dallas*. In spite of this being a hit show, I had still had some remnants of theater snobbery. Creatively, I thought I was slumming.

When I showed up for my first day of shooting, leading man Larry Hagman came up and introduced himself. We didn't have any scenes together, and he could have invoked his star status and ignored me all week. Instead, he smiled broadly and said, "Hi, Michael. I'm Larry. Welcome to *Dallas*. You'll find that we aren't particularly 'good' here, but we are very successful. Have a great week and welcome aboard. Let us know if you need anything."

I've never forgotten his friendliness and generosity toward a newcomer. I learned that hit shows are usually happy sets, where people are actually enjoying themselves. Shows that are struggling or failing can be very tense sets because everyone from the star to the wardrobe folks know they could be off the lot and looking for their next job any day. I was beginning to think this world of TV wasn't so terrible after all.

But not before I booked a guest-star spot on the hugely successful series *Melrose Place*. I had never seen the show, and really had no interest in it. Vapid. Shallow. Meaningless. I didn't want to spend my time watching *that*. Yet here I was, arriving for my first day on the set. I had babies at home and bills to pay.

As the second assistant director led me to my dressing room, we crossed the soundstage with a massive set: a huge apartment-building courtyard, complete with swimming pool, lounge chairs, and palm trees. I marveled to the AD, "This is amazing. What is this?"

She looked at me blankly. "This is Melrose Place."

Ouch. I didn't have to be a fan of the show, but I should have at least been smart (and respectful) enough to recognize its world. In the end, *Melrose Place* was a very happy set on which to work, everyone from top to bottom terrific at their jobs and focused on the same goal.

If you consider some of the jobs you might be getting to be a form of creative slumming, you should still respect the opportunity and understand the world into which you've been invited. Actors always talk about "the work" being so important. It is. But sometimes "the work" is simply... work. And there's absolutely nothing wrong with that. Be respectful, be grateful, and you might learn something new.

REPRESENTATION: WHO'S RIGHT FOR YOU?

It's no secret that excellent representation is key to taking your talent to the marketplace. And there's no shortage of books and resources concerned with finding agents and managers. If you were resourceful enough to find me and find this book, you most likely know the "how" of getting representation. But I will say a few things about the "who."

When it comes to getting a great agent or manager, it is who you know. That "who" should be:

- someone who's in alignment with your hopes and dreams;
- someone who's further up the food chain than you are;
- someone who truly "gets" you;
- someone who's honest; and
- someone who's dedicated to working hard for your success.

Artists throughout the history of the world have needed people of influence to act on their behalf. Art dealer Theo van Gogh was crucial to Vincent's progress. Picasso and Matisse were connected with wealthy collectors thanks to Gertrude Stein. Today's reps, even the sharks that fit the popular image of *Entourage*'s Ari Gold, are heirs to a long tradition of connecting talent with opportunity.

AGENT? MANAGER? OR BOTH?

Like a lot of what has changed for actors going from the 20th to 21st century, representation is in a state of flux. Today, there are agents who stay small and function more like managers. And many managers are former agents. The line blurs more and more every year. So do you need both?

Many actors function perfectly fine with one and not the other. That said, I always think it's better to have more than one entity working on your behalf. And if a representative is part of a large management company with production arms, literary departments, game-design departments, and other capabilities, that means more opportunity for you. Here are the practical differences:

Contracts: Agents can legally negotiate your union contracts. Managers cannot, although they do it all the time (wink, wink).

Clients: In general, but not always, agents have more clients, and managers fewer. Whether you're one of hundreds or one of a handful translates into the amount of attention you can command.

Percentages: Agents take 10% of your earnings. Managers, being unregulated, can take whatever you agree to (10% to 15% is the norm).

So do you need *both* agent and manager? The bottom line is that you need people who share your hopes and dreams, and you need people of influence. An agent or manager alone may answer this requirement. It could take both, working in tandem. The fit of your needs and their skills will determine that.

You've heard the cliché: "I'll have my people talk to your people." **You need people. Good people.**

5 TIPS FOR WORKING WITH REPRESENTATIVES

So what's next? You just sit by the phone and wait for those calls, right? No. That's last century's business model. Today's Authentic Actor must be a creative force in building his or her own momentum. Passivity is so passé.

Your team of representatives may include an agent, manager, publicist, and / or lawyer. But your team is just that: *your* team. They should be as hungry to build your career as you are. If you're not getting sent out for roles that fit you — or if you're not getting sent out at all — it's time to have a frank chat (or maybe even fire them).

Before that level of frustration sets in, however, resolve to build a constructive relationship by keeping your people involved. If it's slow, find reasons to send a weekly email (or phone call) about what you're up to: a play reading, a short film you're writing, an improv class you're taking. Invite them to see you work, wherever that may be. They may or may not be able to come, but this helps create the narrative that you are busy, creatively engaged, and continually working.

The old adage "out of sight, out of mind" is absolutely true in this business. Stay on their radar; that's part of your job. Here are a few tips:

1. **How much is too much?** Be sensitive to that fine line between staying in touch and bugging them too much. If you're not sure where it is, don't be afraid to ask.

2. **Get interested in them as people.** Find out what activities their kids are into. Do you have interests in common (other than building your career)? Find out their birthdays. Send handwritten notes rather than emails or texts. Cards are personal, and this is a personal business.

3. Show your gratitude. Their job is difficult. They're on the receiving end of rejection as much as actors are, and the best of them take it as hard as some of their clients do. Thank them for their efforts when it makes sense.

4. Ask for what you need. If you're not getting what you need, give them a nudge.

5. Invest your time and attention. It's just like any other relationship you value. Taking care of your connections will help them to grow.

THE PERSONAL TOUCH

We are engaged in an artistic endeavor and a business that feeds heavily on the interplay between personal and professional relationships. In this effort, no one functions in a vacuum. It's all about people. And it's a business that thrives on the personal touch. **It's not show business. It's human business.**

There's an apocryphal story about Marlon Brando when he was a struggling young actor in New York, before his star rose through *A Streetcar Named Desire*. When the weather was particularly horrible (whether drenching rain or a snowstorm), he would make a special effort to go on his rounds of visiting agents and casting directors. His logic was that he would be the one actor so dedicated he'd show up whatever the weather was. He'd be memorable. A smart strategy — and highly personal.

A young actress in my class was casting her net wide in an attempt to obtain a good manager to represent her. She mentioned in class that she was going to send email thank-you's to those who had responded. My advice? Send the real thing, handwritten, stamped, and sent via snail mail. Emails are deleted at lightning speed, but what we hold in our hands stands a chance of being remembered. The personal touch has even more value in our virtual and digital age. Handwriting expresses who you are, as do your words and the type of notecard you choose to send.

Old fashioned? Perhaps. But also the mark of a class act. As a young actor, I had the pleasure and the privilege of guest-starring on many shows produced by Steven Bochco, one of the great forces in modern television. Bochco was responsible for many landmark shows including *Hill Street Blues*, *L.A. Law*, and *NYPD Blue*. Here's the deal: Steven always sent you a personally handwritten note when your episode aired. It was from him to you, and he always included some specific praise for your work and gratitude for your contribution to the show.

One of the biggest producers in television took the time to send every guest actor a personal note! That definitely made an impression on me. He also always made it a point to be at every audition, even for the smallest parts (yes, there *are* small parts). This was a guy who had his fingerprints on everything, and it showed in the quality of his work and in the loyalty of people who worked with him year in and year out — a team drawn together through that personal touch.

FROM YOUR REP'S POINT OF VIEW

At a basic level, an agent and manager should identify opportunities for you as an actor and secure appointments for those opportunities. They should also provide expert advice on the fine art of career strategy. They succeed when you succeed.

But consider this: Your new agent or manager has offices at 9200 Sunset Boulevard in West Hollywood, a good address with very high rent. He used to have seven clients on network TV series. He now has two. In the breakdowns he sees a lot of ultra-low-budget films that pay actors $100 per day. He's feeling the squeeze, just like we all are.

When agents look at an actor, they either see dollar signs or they don't. It's not personal. They're in the *business* part of show business. The best ones also understand and respect your artistic life, but they too have rent to pay, kids to put through school — a life to support.

What has happened to our business very much mirrors what has happened to our country and culture: There is huge money at the top and very little left for anyone else. This is the new normal. Try to understand the pressures in her or his life and career as well. That person is your partner, and you are not the only one under the gun. You aren't the only one striving for grace under adverse conditions.

EVERYONE LIES

My apologies to the many wonderful agents and managers in my career, but to some extent it's true: Everyone lies — including us actors. Most lies are small. To secure an appointment, an agent or manager may lie on your behalf about how much interest other casting directors are taking in you. An actor may lie about how well he thought an audition went. We don't want to disappoint our reps. They don't want to kill our confidence or stall our momentum.

In the entertainment business, most lies of this kind aren't malicious or manipulative. They're something more like wishful thinking or optimism. *If I say it, it will be true.* **So much of what we do is an exercise in self-confidence. Sometimes the line between confident self-talk and overblowing reality can be a thin one.** Most of us in this situation aren't really lying. We're just saying something that's not quite true — yet.

Let's say you get a great appointment. Your agent says she got it for you (and really had to pitch hard for it). Your manager says that he got it for you (he knows the series producer personally). Who's taking credit where it's not due? The bottom line is that you got the appointment. Don't waste time trying to figure out who's being more truthful. Just go out and put your name on that role.

These are small lies, and I say ignore them as long as you are all moving forward together. There are, however, those whoppers that are cut-and-dried, out-and-out dishonesty. One of my representatives once told me a huge lie. When I discovered it, there was only one choice: He had to go because I could no longer trust him.

Trust is key. When a lie shakes the trust in your working relationship, it's time to fire that rep. Representatives don't have to be your best friend. They don't have to be people you really want to hang with. If it turns out that they are, that's a little added bonus. But they need to "get" you. They need to be on the path with you, and you must be able to trust them.

LETTING A REP GO

Firing your agent or manager is always tough. It's like breaking up with someone, and the anticipation of that difficult confrontation is brutal. In spite of that, it's best to do it face to face, or (at a minimum) over a phone call.

Sometimes the air has become so toxic that a phone call is preferable to the face-to-face meeting — but that meeting is the right thing to do, always. Follow it up with a hard-copy letter, mailed to the rep's office, simply stating that you are terminating the relationship.

A text or email is never the right way to handle this situation. Despite everything, this is someone who has worked on your behalf, in good faith, believing that their investment in time will pay off down the line. You owe them the courtesy of a personal and professional termination of the relationship. It's part of being a grownup.

IT'S ALWAYS BEEN TOUGH.
NOW GET ON WITH IT.

Nostalgia is very seductive. The past is always a safe refuge. We observe the past through rose-colored glasses. Our selective memories often have us only remembering how wonderful things were. But the reality is more complex, more varied, and invariably less rosy.

No one can fail to notice our deeply ailing world. Historically, there have always been times of bad news, hopelessness, disaster. The end of the world has been just around the corner ever since humans first became capable of rational thought. Those good old days were also wreathed in doom and gloom. Nostalgia is seductive, especially when we think about our own lives and careers.

A friend offered some unsolicited advice to me about how to speak to the young actors that I teach and coach. He said, "Be brutal with them. Tell it like it is. Tell them that if they can do anything else, they should."

I'm not exactly sure what this sledgehammer approach accomplishes. That advice would certainly have rolled off my back when I was young. I was not going to be discouraged. Hope and encouragement are among the traits the young actor needs in order to go out and tilt at windmills. And that kind of advice always rings of bitterness, a reflection of someone whose dreams remain unfulfilled. Not my style; I am not in the discouragement business. While I won't give false encouragement to someone who clearly doesn't have what it takes, I have seen enough improbable success stories to be humbled. One person's opinion is just that: one person's opinion.

The entertainment business is always in the middle of the best and the worst of times. Even during the so-called golden eras of the past, the next looming innovation was always threatening what was working at the moment. The advent of sound, of television (then color TV), of the Internet — all of these were exciting for people who could see opportunities in the changes. Others could only see what they might lose — money, status, and a sense of mastery over a business that is never certain. I hear over and over:

"You can't make a living in this business anymore. You might make a killing, but you can't make a living."

"You should have been in this business 30 years ago. It was run by showmen, not accountants."

"Talent means nothing anymore."

"It used to be fun, it used to have heart, it used to mean something."

"Standards have fallen. Now anything passes for talent."

"There's nothing good out there."

For the record: These were all things that I heard over 30 years ago when I started out in the business. Everything old is new again. I observed older actors who were bitter and closed off to the changes around them, and I vowed to never wander into that neighborhood.

"Tell it like it is; be brutal," my friend had suggested. I do believe in being realistic, but imparting pessimism is like spreading the flu. It takes hold, and nothing really good comes of it. There's simply no point in discouraging those who cannot be discouraged. And, by the way, it's precisely the ones who cannot be discouraged who have a real chance of success.

But let's be completely honest: If you consider the odds of success in this pursuit every morning before you have your coffee, you'll never leave the house. It's a very tough business. It is unforgiving, unfair, fickle, heartbreaking, dream-crushing, mean, myopic, and merciless. It's all true — every bit of it. However what's also true is that this endeavor has the potential to be inspiring, fulfilling, educating, brilliant, fun, and life-affirming. That's also all true — every bit of it. Which narrative you choose is very much up to you.

KNOW WHEN TO SAY "FUCK 'EM"

A steady diet of audition rejections can demoralize even the most committed actor. Instead of becoming bitter about not getting the nod, actors I admire continue to find new ways to stay creatively active and viable. It's never been easier for actors to produce and distribute their own work; new technologies have greatly democratized the process of creating a product. Anyone with an iPad and an idea can create content. Every day more people are collaborating and connecting to keep their respective dreams alive and viable.

Meanwhile, the wheels of the entertainment industry continue to inexorably grind away and could possibly be headed in your direction on any given day. It's the Wild West out there, and don't expect the dust to settle anytime soon. The only constant is change, which you can weather with consistent dedication, passion, and belief in yourself.

This is the nature of the business, and it's designed to test your confidence. So when things aren't going your way, I say, *fuck 'em!* Just keep working. Keep exploring. Decide that you are in this for the long haul. Find your artistic community, and eventually that "other way" they go will lead them right to you. The real you.

7

THE BUSINESS OF LIFE

You are an actor, artist, and citizen.

LIFE AS CRAFT

In all things, I believe in craft. I believe in technique. I believe that when those are in place, inspiration (and even those moments of artistic ecstasy) find an open door, a welcoming place, water, and sunshine.

It's imperative that you continue to work at your craft. That's a given, and must be part of your routine. But that aspect of your artistic life cannot exist in a vacuum. You exist in real time, in the world as it is — and hopefully as it may be or should be. You are actors and artists, and you are also citizens. Your job, frankly, is to reflect the world as it continues to change and evolve.

A great deal of acting training creates a hermetically sealed universe that has little connective tissue to the real world around you. It's focused on skills only — not on the imperfect flesh and blood that has to eventually leave the artificial bubble of class, then make the work compelling in an office on a studio lot or in a garage in Burbank, taping a scene that's going to be sent to a producer in New York or New Orleans... who will view it on a smartphone. That's what it really looks like. That's what success, failure, heartbreak, and luck really look like.

It's terribly important to place yourself in the context of what exists, and of what is coming. It's our duty as artists to have our ear to the ground and feel the tremors of what's coming. Remember this: **The only constant is change, and the future will present opportunities that will surprise and delight you — as long as you stay open and engaged in the world at large.**

ENGAGE WITH THE WORLD BEYOND ACTING

You get a role in a big studio movie. What can go wrong? In the case of my role as Adam Sandler's dad in *Just Go With It*, I ended up on the cutting-room floor. Of my twelve days' work, nearly all of it was cut. I was disappointed, but after about 20 minutes I had to decide if I was going to let the disappointment fester. That question and answer are really the only parts of the situation in my control.

Complaining is a bad habit, and I have been guilty of it in the past, so I speak from experience. Talk to an unemployed actor, and you will hear complaining. But if you want to hear *real* complaining, talk to an actor who has a job.

"They have no idea what they are doing!"

"The script sucks."

"They say they have no money, but look what they're spending on the costumes!"

The reality was that I had a great time making the film (with residuals, thank you very much). Adam was wonderful to me, and — hold on — I'm complaining? My mother would say to me when I was a boy, "You'd complain with a loaf of bread under each arm!" She was right. This ain't death or cancer.

The totality of an actor's life can't be just about acting. Do not equate your self-worth solely with your work. As actors, our job is to reflect life and illuminate existence. We can't do that if we only participate in life as actors — if that's the entirety of who we think we are. Volunteer. Plant a garden. Build a cabinet. Do something tangible that expands your imagination and humanity.

Becoming an actor requires the zeal and passion of the amateur and the hard-nosed determination of the professional. But it also means engaging with the world beyond acting. **Develop your talent and your life in tandem. Each is incomplete without the other.**

"Becoming a writer was more important for me psychologically than career-wise, because I wasn't waiting for someone else to give me a way to validate my existence. It lowered the stakes on the acting."

— JIM PIDDOCK, actor / writer / producer

FIND YOUR TRIBE

The period of time between Thanksgiving and the New Year is intense. Parties. Drinking. Food. Family. Friends. This season, while busy, is sort of a large, collective afternoon nap; restorative, yet we wake from it groggy.

After the annual holiday get-together of my students and coaching clients, assorted significant others and spouses, and friends of the enterprise, I realized that this community of people did not exist in this particular way until I created it. This was my doing. And theirs. And I also realized how much my life has been enriched by knowing them, working with them, and helping some of them create their own paths toward artistry, a career, a dream.

Artists need to find their tribe: the film geeks, the singers, the theater kids, the musicians, the "others." It's exciting to discover these connections and communities for the first time. This tribe is definitely a significant part of my larger community. Ours is not a solitary art form. Ours is a handmade art form that is only as strong as the weakest link.

To make your life in the arts requires desire, passion, and commitment. These are the things that bind our tribe together in ways that are unique. The reality is that we live and work in more disconnected ways today. Our daily points of contact can get reduced to the virtual and digital. Although being in virtual touch is a wonderful innovation, it's no substitute for flesh and blood. Spend time face to face, where the unexpected can happen, where friendships and relationships — both personal and professional — are forged.

MY FIRST TRIBE

In 2010, I was on a plane returning from a memorial service for Charles Nolte — actor, director, teacher, friend, playwright, mentor, citizen of the world. Charles was a very bright light for many people and was 87 when he died. He had been a major Broadway star during the late 1940s and 1950s. I knew him as a theater professor at the University of Minnesota and as a director.

His natural energy and passion for the arts made everyone he knew feel as if they alone were his best friend. It's a tribute to Charles that he had many of these best friends, all becoming peers through the osmosis of Charles. We young actors found ourselves in the "company" of Tennessee Williams, Charles Laughton, Katharine Cornell.

All who spoke at the memorial service could mark the moment when knowing Charles had changed their lives. His tribe gathered — people whose lives had been changed by Charles — and gave thanks for his rather grand, long, and joyous life.

I saw faces I hadn't seen in 30 years. We were older but still tied together by a common thread: We had all come of age in the theater together. And, as I looked around the room, it hit me: Outside of my family, *this* was my first tribe. They were there for my most formative experiences. We came of age together. We were young together.

GATHERING A TRIBE

I've been fortunate to do four films with writer / director John Sayles. John and his producer (and wife) Maggie Renzi always make it a point to truly get to know their collaborators personally. As a result, we have been good friends for over 25 years, and you'll see some familiar faces show up in many of their films.

Wherever we shot, they built a creative encampment. They developed relationships with their fellow artists as well as with the community where we were shooting. I met people in Alaska, where we shot *Limbo*, who are still friends. The same can be said for our time shooting *Passion Fish* in Louisiana.

John and Maggie, actors themselves, knew that actors respond well to being treated as collaborators rather than hired help. We give our very best work when we feel invested in a project. It has been my experience that the very best talent — the crème de la crème — are often the most personally dynamic, collaborative, and inspiring individuals. They realize that creating a team where everyone is pulling in the same direction stands a better chance of producing quality results. And if for some reason it does not (no one sets out to make a bad movie, but they do occur on a regular basis), you've at least had a memorable experience along the way.

I try to carry this ethos this into my teaching and coaching. I honestly don't know any other way to do it. Yes, be a good teacher, or — if I can — be a *great* teacher. But also be a reliable ear, a constructive critic, an honest friend, an advisor, and a mentor.

Years later, John and Maggie had a "gathering of the tribe," as they called it, in New Hampshire. More than 200 people from all corners of the world showed up: former cast and crew from many films together with their children, grandchildren, and all sorts of significant others. A tribe of fellow artists, an extended community created through their personal touch.

FIND YOUR TRIBE IN L.A.

Finding your tribe in Los Angeles can be a challenge. I'm a huge fan of L.A. (not always a fashionable opinion in some circles). Unlike New York, the essence of L.A. does not hit you in the face the moment you walk out the door. L.A. is a collection of more than 100 distinctly different neighborhoods. That means you have to go out and find *your* L.A. That finding is the real journey, the real discovery.

If you are an actor in Los Angeles, your tribe is out there waiting for you to find or create. It might be in an acting class. It might be in a voiceover waiting room or a web-series read-through. It might be in a theater company or on a film set. It might be at a church, synagogue, mosque, meditation center, or hiking trail.

It's there. And it's important as artists that we recognize this need and not isolate ourselves. It's easy to become isolated here, but you have a choice. You must choose to go out and find your tribe. Having this significant group of passionate coworkers is absolutely imperative.

Don't isolate. Congregate. Go out and find your tribe.

DIVIDE AND CONQUER

Many actors have to be jugglers. Multiple jobs, multiple projects, multiple priorities. Where to put your energy first? How to get back on track when something goes off the rails? Raising a family while building a career in Hollywood taught me early to divide and conquer. Think about the priorities in your life as distinct silos of thought and action (even though they invariably overlap and blend at times).

If you do not honor these boundaries, one activity will crowd into the other. This is a real problem in a career where disappointment can be an everyday occurrence. One thing going wrong can make you feel like *everything* is going wrong. That makes it tougher to recover and keep moving forward with the rest of what you want and need to get done.

A friend was struggling to find time to put into his acting. After all, he had directing and producing projects, he was writing a screenplay, his personal life was temporarily unsettled, he was waiting for some money to come in... and on and on. It was a jumble of uncertainties that were all beginning to infect each other with stress and negativity.

I advised him to separate these issues — divide and conquer by putting them in different mental silos. Put your most precious resources into quarantine, which helps to create room for success in other areas — areas untouched by adjacent failures that can and do occur.

Bad news is contagious, and it can infect other parts of your life and work. Staying resilient is easier with clear mental boundaries. By seeing your efforts as distinct, fluid parts in a larger whole, when one goes sideways, the others can still keep moving.

PAY YOURSELF FIRST

Many years ago, I engaged a financial advisor. When I expressed to him that I wasn't sure how I could save anything to invest because I had a mortgage, kids, and all the accompanying expenses that come with both, he said very simply, "Pay yourself first." In other words, if you have $5,000, pay yourself $1,000 first. Put that money away in a safe place, forget about it, and find a way to live on the rest.

This was tried-and-true advice, hardly original, yet when I first heard it, it made such simple and ultimate sense. And it works for more than money. Similar to filling a savings account, paying yourself first *creatively* helps to keep that well of inspiration full. Only you can create the time and space in your life for that replenishment to happen — and it has to happen.

A young friend was doing everything he could to juggle all the variables at play in his life: acting, directing, producing, writing, a relationship, finances, and more. This is a very talented and substantial guy who, like so many of us, was trying to create a life based on his passions. Not just a career. A life.

I'm more than a few years down the road from where he is, but I understand the struggle vividly. I'm still in the struggle! I think that if you're not struggling, odds are that you're dead. I told him a simple thing that applies to money and creativity: pay yourself first.

In his case, working on his development as an actor was crucially important to him, yet he made precious little time for it. He found it difficult to justify and fulfill since it wasn't bringing in any money at the moment. Yet this very passion was the foundation of all his other professional efforts and successes.

So that "bank account" has to be replenished. It gets drained from time to time, and it must be refilled so that it can help "pay" for your other creative efforts. It's the headwaters of the river.

These are lessons I learned the hard way — by making *all* of these mistakes at some point in my own creative life. Lessons learned the hard way are always the most resonant: **Make time for the passions that are central to your creativity. Understand that if you don't fund your creative self, no one else will.** Place real tangible value on your creative life. Bank the artistic currency to keep your creative prosperity flowing.

BELIEVE AND MOVE FORWARD

Most who are actors also have to do things that are not exactly what they trained for or wished for. They wait tables, do commercials and voiceovers, work in temp jobs, and accept acting gigs that are far less aspirational than they'd envisioned. There is nothing wrong with good, honest work, but we have to also work at retaining our passion in the face of taking care of the basic necessities of food, clothing, and shelter.

Frankly, I've had long periods of being creatively asleep. Life simply got in the way. When the realities of careers, marriage, kids, mortgages, school tuition, and so much more invade, it can be a near-impossible pivot back to creative fertility. But even in the darkest of my creative times, for some reason I had faith that the artistic flame would reignite. I wasn't sure how or when, but I proceeded as if it would. I went forward on belief.

Now, let's get one thing straight: This was not some sort of heroic endurance on my part. I endured because doing so made the most sense. When I actually sat down and examined my other options, enduring sounded pretty good to me. I give a lot of credit to my wife, Emily, for showing me the wisdom of holding onto this. And I'd had just enough success to tantalize me. I was always encouraged just enough to keep coming back for more. In fact, sometimes I felt I might be living proof of the adage that L.A. is the only place you can die of encouragement.

But this is how careers are made. **Staying with it is the only way you'll be there with an oar in the water when (all of a sudden) people see you in a new light — simply because you're still there.** In the meantime, reconnect with your original impulse. You owe it to yourself and your talent. There is a reason you took this path.

It is incumbent upon all of us to keep our creative flame burning. That may mean taking an acting class, reading more, digging deep into film archives, or writing a short story. Talent does not go away. It simply waits for its day to reemerge.

Into my sixth decade, I actually think my best years are ahead of me. Delusional, you say? It doesn't really matter. I believe it, and it keeps me moving forward.

PLAN FOR CREATIVE RECOVERY

An actor auditioning for a guest-starring role in a TV series came to me for coaching. This is an actor of considerable talent, who had experienced some tough knocks over the past several years, both personal and professional. In the coaching session, he was totally on fire. He was highly connected to this role, in large part because it was a character who had also been wronged and misunderstood — something he could relate to in his own life. The role and his present life were in perfect alignment.

His audition prep before he came to me and during the time we worked was electric. He went into the audition room and did all of that and more. He was told that they loved his work. And... he was also told that they'd made another choice. Every jilted actor has heard all the phrases:

"It's not going forward."

"They felt they had stronger choices."

"It wasn't a good fit."

And the kicker: "They loved you, but they went another way."

They went another way? Which way did they go? Maybe I could meet them there and discuss this?

This is a terribly tough business where your very best work can be met with inane responses that, although often well-meaning, are hurtful, frustrating, disheartening, and simply not useful. He poured his heart into that role and received very good feedback, plus a few clichés thrown in for good measure. You can die from such encouragement.

He sent me an email saying, in part: "Stings a bit, this one. Truth is, I'm a marathon runner. So I'll keep going. Again, much thanks for being a part of my creative recovery."

Creative recovery. Those words really jumped off the page.

Most of us who are (or aspire to be) creative artists go down the rabbit hole from time to time. We lose track of the original impulse to create, to share, to tell stories, to be a part of some higher and dynamic reality and imagination. Life gets in the way sometimes, and we turn away from the flame.

I have had my own detours from the creative life, but always seem to find my way back. Sometimes you do need a guide, a "creative Sherpa" to help you along. Jeffrey Tambor was that for me at a time when I needed it. He pushed me (while I resisted) back onto the path — and for that I will always be grateful. He knew something I didn't: that I needed a push at just that moment. Just as I knew something that my very talented client didn't: that he needed to be reminded of his talent. He needed genuine encouragement, based on the resonance of his work. He felt creatively alone, in a vacuum, which is a tough place to find your own way out of.

Of course it would have been sweeter had he booked the job. "It's an honor just to be nominated," right? Bullshit! We all want to be picked. Let's own up to that. It's human nature. But rediscovering his creative force had to be reward enough for the moment.

I've often joked that I should create a 12-Step Program for actors who can't take it anymore. The scene might look something like this:

```
INT. ACTORS ANONYMOUS MEETING IN
PROGRESS

ME: Hi. My name is Michael, and I'm
an actor.

THE GROUP: Hi, Michael.

ME: I was so happy to find a meeting
here in Studio City. (pause) Well...
good news. I turned down two auditions
this week!
```

```
            (murmurs of approval and
            encouragement)

Whew. Not easy, right? That's actually
kind of hard to even say out loud.

            (pause — then proudly)

I've been audition-free for 8 months,
2 weeks, 3 days, and 6 hours.

THE GROUP: (cheers) Awesome, Michael!
Stay strong! We're here for you!
```

We *all* get lost from time to time. Make it a priority to find your way back, creating time and space in your life for that process. Seek out and find a guide to your creative recovery. Reconnect to the hard work and creativity that can soften the slights and align you with your original impulse to do this. It's the art of walking back into the flame with purpose, talent, and hope.

REMIND YOURSELF OF YOUR TALENT

A very good actress once told me, "The only acting I'm doing these days is at auditions." She wasn't happy about it, but it was her creative life in a nutshell. No classes, no workshops, no improv, no working on stage — just auditions.

If an actor wants a surefire way of taxing her immune system and coming down with the virus of self-doubt — especially a young, developing actor — this would be it. Auditions are rarely conducive to showcasing one's full talent. It's like a marathon runner only doing 20-yard sprints!

When I was younger I was always onstage, working in plays. It was the most dynamic way that I knew of to learn my craft, sharpen my acting instincts, and stay connected to my talent. Other actors I know create short films, write and play music, paint, get inspired at art museums, or volunteer in their community.

Creativity is multidimensional. Exercise yours in as many ways as you can. The first step into the unknown is always the most difficult, but untold rewards are waiting if you take it.

AS GOOD AS THE BEST THING YOU'VE EVER DONE

While doing some paperwork at home, I had the TV on. Turner Classic Movies makes very good background noise, but my attention sharpened when an interstitial TCM original biography, *Jack Lemmon on Billy Wilder*, came on the screen. Legendary writer / director Billy Wilder was a seven-time Oscar winner and creator of films including *Sunset Boulevard*, *Some Like It Hot*, *The Apartment*, and *The Lost Weekend*.

Film footage of Wilder receiving his AFI Life Achievement Award showed him speaking with undiminished, razor-sharp wit about art, life, and the state of the film business. A Jew who fled Nazi-occupied Europe, his worldview was deeply informed by that experience, his body of work laced with irony, wit, depth, and a puckish sense of humor.

Jack Lemmon talked about how much Wilder meant to him as a mentor, friend, and fellow artist. Lemmon remembered Wilder telling him, "Remember, you are as good as the best thing you've ever done."

That simply stopped me cold. A powerful concept that is easy to lose sight of, especially in tough times. Artistic lives ebb and flow, and when we're in the inevitable ebb phase, our go-to psychological position can be bleak. I certainly have done my time in "I'll-never-work-again" hell. Precisely at these junctures, remembering the value of our very best work is terribly important. In fact, it's crucial.

Wilder lived to be 95 in a town and an industry that worships youth — always has and likely always will. He made his last real feature at age 75, and it was not a success. He tried for many years to get another film, but never succeeded. I often saw him in Beverly Hills, out and about, a vigorous man who was still sharp, clever, and engaged in life. I feel certain that what he said to Jack Lemmon was something he also privately said to himself and about himself.

His place in the pantheon of cinema history was secure, but he still wanted to work. He still had stories to tell. Conventional wisdom was that he had lost it — whatever "it" is. We will never know if he had another great film in him (I suspect he did). But I have to believe that he never lost sight of this core value: **You're as good as the best thing you've ever done.**

Keep that in mind as you move forward. Do work that makes you proud. Embrace failure when it happens. Learn from it. And when times get tough, as they inevitably will, remember — you're as good as the best thing you've ever done.

HOLD IT RIGHT HERE

Actor Ron Perlman once said to my students, "You have to hold it right here," gesturing with great purpose to an aspirational spot just above his eyeline, out toward the horizon. He was talking about how we need to see and approach our artistic lives.

He recounted a time when he was younger and getting absolutely nowhere in his career or artistic life. At that impressionable moment, he saw the great Irene Worth in *Sweet Bird of Youth*. Her performance was, for him at that crucial juncture, a gigantic artistic peak that gave him something to reach for.

He said, "I knew that if I could have even a small part of what she accomplished that night, I'd crawl through whatever I needed to to be able to affect people like that."

ACTING AS CALLING

Imagine yourself in subfreezing temperatures managing cast, crew, teams of racing sled dogs, and two thousand extras. It took all that over two days to get a single shot in the feature film *Iron Will*. In the midst of this barely controlled madness, the director Charlie Haid turned to me and said, "Why did we all decide to do this again?" We shared a knowing laugh, understanding that sometimes in the midst of the craziness, when the momentum of a production is raging around you, it all seems absolutely impossible — yet we do it and hunger to do it again.

I ask my students the same question: Why did they decide to take up this near-impossible pursuit? The answer is uniform: Nothing is as exciting. Nothing lights them up in the same way. Nothing compares to how it feels when it's good. This is, in some way, a calling. Authentic Actors, every one of them.

RENEW YOUR CREATIVE VOWS

At their wedding-anniversary party, my sister and her husband renewed their marriage vows. It's one thing to know what's in your heart; it's quite another to say it out loud it in front of friends and family. It clarifies. It distills. It leaves no doubt.

It occurred to me that **as artists, we need to renew our vows to ourselves, to declare what we are about, to restate our dedication and devotion to this pursuit we chose.** This is a very difficult choice we have made, and it seems appropriate to renew that vow from time to time. Take a full measure of yourself — rededicate your passion, engagement, and focus.

I have certainly had many periods in my career when my dedication waned. Being an artist is a wonderful thing in a vacuum, but the business part of being an actor is often fraught with compromises and disappointments. My IMDb page shows a tangible record of work, but it doesn't show the struggle. From the outside looking in, it appears calm and accomplished. From the inside, it's been more like a fight — get that audition, lose jobs to those actors on the "lists," hope that the luck I saw bestowed on others would one day shine on me. It's a tough gig we have chosen, and it certainly can test your dedication.

Every so often the renewable option on our heart and soul comes up for review. It's at that juncture that we should formally renew our vows to ourselves. Put your stakes on the table again. Remember the moments that made you see a new level of aspiration for your own life. Reacquaint yourself with the Authentic Actor in you... yourself. Our passion is the ultimate renewable resource.

GURU IN THE MIRROR

An old and dear friend told me a story that went like this: As a 13-year-old about to have his bar mitzvah, he was looking forward to one moment in particular. He had seen and been fascinated by the special time near the end of the ceremony when the rabbi whispered something quietly to the boy or girl — a special message that no one else could hear.

My friend, thinking the secret of life was about to be imparted to him, was waiting for his whispered moment. It finally came. The rabbi approached him. *This is it!* The rabbi leaned in quietly, and with great import, whispered, "Good luck."

Good luck? That's it? *Good luck?* To say my friend was disillusioned would be an understatement. Lots of hard work and spiritual investment for... *good luck?* My friend was probably lucky that at age 13, his disillusionment was so complete that he began a lifelong search for meaning. He was hoping that the rabbi was going to be his guru, his spiritual guide.

If you are searching for a guru, you will eventually find one. The line between guru and mentor can be hard to recognize. I believe we need mentors — creative Sherpas. You need a certain level of maturity and self-awareness to benefit from a guru. You need the inner fortitude to take what works for *you* and to discard the narcissism that is sometimes part of a guru's motivation.

When we train as artists, we all need guidance. Attaining artistry is not a linear path. It's rarely obvious what the next step should be. Everyone carves their own unique road map, and seeking out a mentor along the way is sometimes part of that process. But be aware that mentors can be gurus as well.

And most gurus are talented and charismatic — or they wouldn't be thought of as gurus. Many acting teachers, some wonderfully talented, fit this profile. The pitfall is that as students, the work can become tied to pleasing the guru, seeking validation. We see our worth reflected in how the guru regards us.

This is a dangerous place, particularly for the formative artist. Encounters between a guru and a fully developed actor who has a strong sense of self (and self-knowledge) can be fruitful. But it's easy for young artists to evaluate their work based solely on the guru's reactions. This is an emotional and artistic cul-de-sac. Some gurus encourage this; at its worst, overreliance becomes a codependent relationship that benefits the guru more than the student.

The real guru in our lives is looking back at us in the mirror every morning — fresh, new, unsullied by the day. Each day is an opportunity to shed the things you want to shed, to assume the new attributes you desire. *We* must each do this; *we* must each put in the time. *We* must pursue self-discovery and lead an examined life — no matter what that journey reveals. *We* must have the endurance and fortitude to keep at it and grow. No one else can do that for us. Seeking this elsewhere will only work if you've already done the inner work.

My goal is for actors to become their own gurus. This doesn't necessarily mean going it alone in a tough business. It does mean learning skills and approaches that put you in control of your artistic future and (as much as possible) your career.

Ironically, the advice my friend's rabbi gave might ultimately be the best message any of us could receive. Good luck is a larger part of success than most of us are willing to admit. My wish for you all is that you create your own unique creative road map and that along the way you have an abundance of good luck.

WHAT DOES SUCCESS LOOK LIKE NOW?

In the first part of this book, I asked you to think about what success looks like in your life and career. Now that we've made our way through art and craft, business and life, has your idea of success changed? Remember: Intention comes from clarity. And action follows intention.

Take a few minutes to look back at what you wrote about what success looks like to you. Does it still combine the best of what you know and feel about what you want from your career and life? Is it the natural result of the advice the guru in the mirror is giving you?

Revisit this exercise to keep your feet on the ground. Do it every year, every six months, or more often... whatever it takes to keep you focused on what makes all the craziness of a life in acting worth it.

YOU'RE GOING TO BE GREAT

When I coach actors for film and TV opportunities, the very last thing I do before they head out the door is this: I look them in the eye and say, "You're going to be great."

I absolutely mean it. In the interest of complete disclosure, some actors are far more capable of being great than others. We all do the best we can, and then we hope for the light in the room to hit us at just the right angle, for the traffic and parking to be trouble-free, for the "audition gods" to smile that day, and for the room we are entering to be friendly and receptive.

I have seen (and been a part of) enough improbable success stories when it comes to casting that I think "you're going to be great" is the best and smartest thing I can say. I quietly utter this confirming mantra to all those going out into the world to slay dragons. It's my version of the thumbs-up before they metaphorically parachute from the plane.

When all is said and done in the strange minefield known as film and TV auditions, **true confidence and your indelible self trump talent most of the time**, like it or not. The reality is that most everyone who makes their way into a casting session has talent, but very few have real confidence. Very few understand their own personal indelibility — their unique presence that can change a room. This is, by definition, more intangible than the strategic work on a scene. But once an actor understands and can embody his or her blink-of-an-eye factor — those magic seconds after we cross the threshold — true confidence is attainable.

But remember this: Confidence is absolutely contagious. It relaxes and reassures. When we are surrounded by people with true confidence, it says to us, "Don't worry. I've got this."

Gaining real confidence doesn't happen on its own or right away. It's a conscious effort, and it must be part of your daily routine until it becomes a part of you. Retaining this confidence in the face of setbacks is a challenge to be met every day. Trying to teach this elusive state of mind is always tricky, always challenging. Everyone is unique; we are all wired differently. Some of us simply can't be held back, and others are constantly wounded and certain that no one "gets" them.

Here's the deal: **They'll never "get" you until** *you* **"get" you.** Until you are comfortable and happy with who you are and can bring that confidence into the room, you are holding yourself back. You are the answer. Many people are never able to grasp this, and give up.

So, after you've put in the time, worked your ass off to get where you are, earned your way into this game — and it is a game with an enormous amount of luck involved — just remember this: **You're going to be great.**

SUMMARY

TODAY'S AUTHENTIC ACTOR

Actors who are making the most of today's entertainment opportunities see their talent holistically and are propelled forward with drive, creativity, imagination, and a personal sense of storytelling. They see themselves as hyphenates: actor-writer, actor-director, actor-producer... but first and foremost, actor-artist.

WHO ARE YOU?

When you clearly communicate and embody your personal fingerprint, you can become unforgettable — indelible. So, you truly need to "get" yourself before you can expect others to "get" you. That means developing your own worldview, and understanding and embracing what is unique in you.

WHAT DO YOU KNOW?

Acting is process, not "how to." Your artistic standards and love of the craft keep you connected to the inner creative drive that sustains professional life. Begin with the text. Create your own road map for the scene. Be inspired by your artistic superheroes and recognize on whose shoulders you stand. Know what you know, and then learn more.

SUCCESS FACTORS

For actors, talent is just the price of admission. Locating and trusting your instinct, facing your fears, and getting specific about goals set the stage for success. That includes becoming more entrepreneurial in the new creative landscape.

THE AUDITION

Auditions are the actor's chance to leave an indelible impression — showing *who you are* as well as *what you can do.* This means using the road map you've created for your scene to give you the courage and confidence to be yourself.

THE ART OF CAREER

Show business has always been tough, but professional actors realize it's not personal. Learn how to stay motivated in the face of rejection and make the most of success. Choose your representatives wisely and manage those relationships with a personal touch. Know what you're worth, and know when to draw the line.

THE BUSINESS OF LIFE

Actors reflect the world, so be part of it. Find your tribe, develop a plan for creative recovery and renewal, and remember why you wanted to pursue this calling in the first place. You're always as good as the best thing you've ever done.

REFERENCES

Clurman, Harold. *The Fervent Years: The Group Theatre and the Thirties*, Da Capo Press, New York, 1983.

Grissom, James. "Ruth Gordon: The Power of Intention," *Follies of God*, May 28, 2012, www.jamesgrissom.blogspot.com/2012/05/ruth-gordon-power-of-intention.html

Perlman, Ron. Interview with author. Pico Playhouse, Los Angeles, CA, May 18, 2011.

Piddock, Jim. Interview with author. Pico Playhouse, Los Angeles, CA, September 18, 2013.

Piznarski, Mark. Interview with author. Pico Playhouse, Los Angeles, CA, March 20, 2013.

Ross, Gary. Interview with author. Pico Playhouse, Los Angeles, CA, March 20, 2014.

Tambor, Jeffrey. Interview with author. Pico Playhouse, Los Angeles, CA, May 19, 2010.

Zane, Debra. Interview with author. Pico Playhouse, Los Angeles, CA, September 10, 2014.

ABOUT THE AUTHOR

Rena Colette Photography, www.renacolette.com

MICHAEL LASKIN has been a working professional actor for more than 35 years in film and television, off-Broadway, at America's leading regional theaters, and in thousands of voiceovers for radio, TV, and animation. He has worked with many of the world's greatest actors, directors, writers, cinematographers, and producers including Robert Duvall, John Sayles, Paul Mazursky, Ben Affleck, Johnny Depp, Jeff Goldblum, Haskell Wexler, Jerry Seinfeld, Kevin Spacey, Alec Baldwin, Barry Levinson, Steven Bochco, Stan Margulies, Stephen Frears, Stanley Tucci, Jeffrey Tambor, James Caan, Tracey Ullman, and Michael Douglas.

As a respected teacher and sought-after acting coach, Michael works with a diverse array of up-and-coming and established actors. Michael and his wife, Emily, live in Studio City, where they raised their two sons, Nick and Joe.

Michael Laskin Studio
Los Angeles, California
www.michaellaskinstudio.com

DIRECTING ACTORS
CREATING MEMORABLE PERFORMANCES
FOR FILM AND TELEVISION

JUDITH WESTON

BEST SELLER
OVER 45,000 COPIES SOLD!

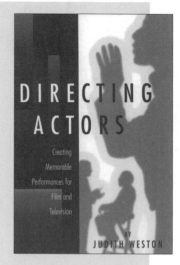

Directing film or television is a high-stakes occupation. It captures your full attention at every moment, calling on you to commit every resource and stretch yourself to the limit. It's the white-water rafting of entertainment jobs. But for many directors, the excitement they feel about a new project tightens into anxiety when it comes to working with actors.

This book provides a method for establishing creative, collaborative relationships with actors, getting the most out of rehearsals, troubleshooting poor performances, giving briefer directions, and much more. It addresses what actors want from a director, what directors do wrong, and constructively analyzes the director-actor relationship.

"Judith Weston is an extraordinarily gifted teacher."
　　　　　　— David Chase, Emmy® Award-Winning Writer,
　　　　　　　Director, and Producer *The Sopranos*,
　　　　　　　Northern Exposure, I'll Fly Away

"I believe that working with Judith's ideas and principles has been the most useful time I've spent preparing for my work. I think that if Judith's book were mandatory reading for all directors, the quality of the director-actor process would be transformed, and better drama would result."
　　　　　　— John Patterson, Director
　　　　　　　Six Feet Under, CSI: Crime Scene Investigation,
　　　　　　　The Practice, Law and Order

"I know a great teacher when I find one! Everything in this book is brilliant and original and true."
　　　　　　— Polly Platt, Producer, *Bottle Rocket*
　　　　　　　Executive Producer, *Broadcast News, The War of the Roses*

JUDITH WESTON was a professional actor for 20 years and has taught Acting for Directors for over a decade.

$26.95 · 314 PAGES · ORDER NUMBER 4RLS · ISBN: 0941188248

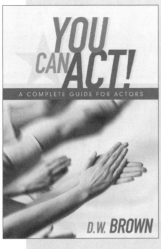

D.W. BROWN

YOU CAN ACT!
A COMPLETE GUIDE FOR ACTORS

D.W. BROWN

What do Jamie Kennedy, Keanu Reeves, Sean Penn, Dustin Hoffman, and Robert DeNiro have in common? They were all coached by or participated in seminars with D.W. Brown — master acting teacher.

You Can Act! describes, with humor and inspiration, every detail necessary for fulfilling any role you might be called upon to perform. Beyond that, it provides extensive tips and reference material for many specialized situations, whether playing comedy or negotiating all manner of stage business; performing the part of a character with insanity or one with a gunshot wound. *You Can Act!* also offers a philosophical approach to performing that unites you with the artists through the ages.

"Working with D .W. Brown is the most important thing I have done for my career. D. W. has a gentle, disarming way about him which helped me break down my social veneers and limitations, and allowed me to expand my capabilities as an actress. This method gave me a road map to follow and all of the tools I needed to continue to develop my instincts so I could take on any role and feel confident about it."
> — Sharon Case, *The Young and the Restless*, five time nominated and winner of the Daytime Emmy for Outstanding Supporting Actress

"D. W. Brown trains beginning actors and makes them working actors, and he takes working actors and makes them stars."
> — Valerie McCaffrey, Head of Casting for New Line Cinema

As artistic head of The Joanne Baron/ D. W. Brown Studio (*www.baronbrown.com*), D. W. BROWN has trained, directed, and coached hundreds of actors and led seminars on acting with Sean Penn, Benicio Del Toro, Anthony Hopkins, Dustin Hoffman, Susan Sarandon, and Sidney Pollack; other notables who have spoken at the studio include Robert De Niro, Jim Caviezel, Jeff Goldblum, Martin Sheen, Richard Dreyfuss, John Singleton, Martha Coolidge, Robert Towne, and Mark Rydell.

D. W. has personally coached and taught Robin Wright Penn, Leslie Mann, Keanu Reeves, Michael Richards, Jamie Kennedy, Nicollette Sheridan, Michael Vartan, Jenny Garth, directors Sam Raimi and Tom Shadyac, and many other great talents. He has just finished writing and directing the feature film *In Northwood* starring Nick Stahl, Olivia Wilde, Dash Mihok, Pruit Taylor Vince, and Shoreh Aghdashloo (Academy® Award nominee for *House of Sand and Fog*).

$24.95 · 350 PAGES · ORDER NUMBER 126RLS · ISBN: 9781932907568

THE MYTH OF MWP

In a dark time, a light bringer came along, leading the curious and the frustrated to clarity and empowerment. It took the well-guarded secrets out of the hands of the few and made them available to all. It spread a spirit of openness and creative freedom, and built a storehouse of knowledge dedicated to the betterment of the arts.

The essence of the Michael Wiese Productions (MWP) is empowering people who have the burning desire to express themselves creatively. We help them realize their dreams by putting the tools in their hands. We demystify the sometimes secretive worlds of screenwriting, directing, acting, producing, film financing, and other media crafts.

By doing so, we hope to bring forth a realization of 'conscious media' which we define as being positively charged, emphasizing hope and affirming positive values like trust, cooperation, self-empowerment, freedom, and love. Grounded in the deep roots of myth, it aims to be healing both for those who make the art and those who encounter it. It hopes to be transformative for people, opening doors to new possibilities and pulling back veils to reveal hidden worlds.

MWP has built a storehouse of knowledge unequaled in the world, for no other publisher has so many titles on the media arts. Please visit www.mwp.com where you will find many free resources and a 25% discount on our books. Sign up and become part of the wider creative community!

Onward and upward,

Michael Wiese
Publisher/Filmmaker